The Constitutional Process in Canada

Two week loan

Please return on or before the last date stamped below.
Charges are made for late return.

McGraw-Hill Ryerson Series in Canadian Politics

Paul W. Fox, *General Editor*

Politics: Canada, 3rd ed.   Paul W. Fox
Canadian Foreign Policy   D.C. Thomson & R.F. Swanson
The Constitutional Process in Canada, 2nd ed.
R.I. Cheffins & R.N. Tucker
Political Party Financing in Canada   K.Z. Paltiel
One Man–One Vote   W.E. Lyons
Nationalism in Canada   P. Russell
Political Parties and Ideologies in Canada
W. Christian & C. Campbell
Canada: A Socio-Political Report   R. Manzer
Pressure Group Behaviour in Canadian Politics   A. Paul Pross
Canada in Question: Federalism in the Seventies   D.V. Smiley
Canadian Political Parties   C. Winn & J. McMenemy

Forthcoming

Canada in Question: Federalism in the Seventies, 2nd ed.
D.V. Smiley
Canadian Politics: Exercises in Analysis   J. Jenson & B. Tomlin
Politics: Canada, 4th ed.   Paul W. Fox
Government in Canada   T.A. Hockin

The Constitutional Process in Canada

Second Edition

R. I. Cheffins
of the Bar of British Columbia
Professor of Law
University of Victoria

R. N. Tucker
of the Bar of British Columbia

McGRAW-HILL RYERSON LIMITED

Toronto   Montreal   New York   London   Sydney   Auckland
Johannesburg   Mexico   Panama   Düsseldorf   Singapore
Kuala Lumpur   New Delhi   São Paulo

THE CONSTITUTIONAL PROCESS IN CANADA
Second Edition

ISBN 0-07-082310-3

Printed and Bound in Canada

4 5 6 7 8 9 10   AP   5 4 3 2 1 0 9

Contents

KEY TO ABBREVIATIONS OF LEGAL AND STATUTORY SOURCES LISTED IN REFERENCES

A.C.	Appeal Cases (U.K.)
D.L.R.	Dominion Law Reports
Q.B.	Queen's Bench (Quebec)
Q.B.D.	Queen's Bench Division (U.K.)
R.S.B.C.	Revised Statutes of British Columbia
R.S.C.	Revised Statutes of Canada
R.S.Q.	Revised Statutes of Quebec
S.C.R.	Supreme Court Reports
W.W.R.	Western Weekly Reports

Preface to the Second Edition

When the first edition of this book was published in 1969 the Canadian Constitution was under major review with the object of drafting a new constitutional document. This attempt failed with the rejection of the Canadian Constitutional Charter by the Province of Quebec in 1971. Nevertheless, since 1969 the evolutionary development of the Canadian Constitution has moved at a very rapid pace, and we felt it necessary to revise the book in order to record these important events. Besides the rejection of the Victoria Charter these include: the creation of the Federal Court of Canada, the passage of important amendments changing the jurisdiction of the Supreme Court of Canada, and a number of important decisions with respect to civil liberties, such as the Drybones and Lavell cases. In addition, we have seen the passage of Canada's Official Languages Act and the upholding of its legality by the Supreme Court of Canada. In the vital area of language, the legislature of Quebec has adopted an official language Act making French the official language in the Province. Undoubtedly this statute will come before the courts with respect to its legality. These are just a few of the recent constitutional developments which we felt should be documented in a second edition.

We would like to thank the Research Committee of the University of Victoria for the financial assistance which made this second edition possible. In addition, we are once again grateful to Professor Paul Fox for reading and commenting upon the manuscript.

Once again the role of Mrs. May Watson was invaluable in that she typed all drafts of the manuscript and, with the help of Mrs. Lilian Smirke, prepared the Index.

RONALD I. CHEFFINS

RONALD N. TUCKER

12 May 1975

One

Introduction: Some Political, Constitutional and Legal Issues in Canada

The years since 1960 have produced more demands and pressures for political and constitutional change in Canada than any other period since Confederation. A wide variety of commentators have suggested changes in the constitutional status quo ranging, for example, from the reorganization of the Supreme Court to the reallocation of tax revenues and legislative powers between the federal and the provincial legislatures. It is becoming increasingly imperative that these demands be examined in the light of the existing constitutional structure. Since political institutions usually have some basic reason for their existence and form, these must be compared with and weighed against the demands and reasons for change. The essence of a healthy political system is the extent to which the best aspects of a political institution can be retained while, at the same time, the institution is reformulated to take account of changing demands and expectations on the part of participants within the political system.

The inevitability of social change is easily conceded, but the questions of speed and direction of change are often difficult. Technological and other factors have resulted in increasing stresses on the entire social fabric. One of the chief political cries of our time is to achieve the maximum of individual dignity. People have sought this goal in a variety of ways for centuries. What is significant about our time is that never before have the vast mass of the political citizenry been so conscious of this goal. A variety of methods have been used and theories advanced on how people can enhance their dignity and status. Many persons have been attracted to communism on the theory that it would enable them to acquire greater dignity through being more effective participants in the political process. It is not necessary to elaborate on the disenchantment of many with this ideology as a method of achieving the sense and reality of political participation.

Another method of seeking this goal has been mass participation in nationalist movements seeking either to attain political independence from a colonial power or to conquer other countries in the name of national destiny. There is no doubt that nationalism does bring, and has brought, both temporary and permanent feelings of individual dignity. It has also produced war and tyranny. The liberal-democratic tradition has emphasized the creation of legal protection from state action as a step toward the achievement of political self-respect. Thus man has swung from the mass movement as a means of achieving dignity, to the traditional liberal-democratic position of maximum legal and social protection of the individual from the real or potential pressures of the state. Both processes are being reproduced in Canada.

The essential political issue in Canada is the relationship between French-speaking and English-speaking citizens. Much of Canada's political and legal framework has been directly influenced by the recurring problems occasioned by the existence in the nation of two dissimilar linguistic groups. Canadians have often liked to think that they are virtually unique in this cultural division. It only takes a very cursory examination of the nations of the world to find that a very high proportion of national states have linguistic and cultural difficulties similar to Canada's: for example, Switzerland, Belgium, Yugoslavia, Guyana, Fiji, Malaysia, Formosa, India, and large parts of South America, to name only a few. Even the supposedly homogeneous nation of Great Britain has within its borders nationalist and separatist groups, albeit weak ones, in both Scotland and Wales.

Perhaps one of the paramount political questions of our time is how the various ethnic groups within a sovereign state resolve their political differences. The role of legal techniques as a method of resolving these differences is an important one in the culturally or linguistically divided country. There is no doubt that, in the past decade, demands made by French Canada have produced major changes in the organization and the running of the country. It has been regarded by many as almost axiomatic that power in the modern federal state tends to be centralized. This trend has been observable at certain times in Canadian history, particularly in time of war. The shift, however, is a pendulum swing rather than a consistent trend, and during the Pearson regime the pendulum clearly started swinging back toward the provinces. It is important to consider how far power can shift in either direction between regional and central governments, and still permit a viable federal system. For example, can a central government lose half or more of its income tax raising power and continue to utilize principles of contemporary economics to control economic currents?

Politics and law have often been seen by North Americans as distinct entities, having little in common. Many lawyers have wished to dissociate their discipline entirely from the political process. British lawyers particularly have attempted to isolate law as a discipline, consciously rejecting the notion that the courts have a substantial policy-making role. Much of this attitude has stemmed from the subservient role of British courts to the ultimate will of the legislature. This is not to say that this attitude is necessarily wrong, for the argument can be made that non-elected judicial appointees should not have ultimate authority over the decisions of properly elected officials. Other lawyers have been afraid that if the public were aware of the range of policy choices which judges possess, it would lose confidence in the legal system. The American legal realists rejected this line of thought and stressed the fact that the public should be aware of the human factor in judicial decision-making.

Law, in our view, is that part of the over-all process of political decision-making which has achieved somewhat more technical, more obvious and more clearly defined ground rules than other aspects of politics. It is still, however, an integral subdivision of the over-all political process. The student of politics, law and legal philosophy is concerned, among other things, with the question of allocation of all types of resources, and with questions of the relationships between individual citizens and between the citizen and the state, as well as the relationships between states. The study of the legal and political process in any nation is a study of how decisions are made, who makes them, what the decisions are, how they influence subsequent events, and how alternative decisions might have led to different results.

One of the chief problems in any constitutional system is to decide when decisions should be made within formal legal channels, and when matters should be left to other more informal and usually more flexible arenas. This is one of the things a formal constitutional document attempts to determine. A constitution usually serves a variety of needs. First, it is a badge of nationhood, an indication that the nation has arrived on the national scene fully clothed with the appropriate legal garb. In addition, as already indicated, constitutions set up certain structures and assign them different authority. These structures are usually given such titles as Parliament, Congress, Courts, Executive Officers, Administration. Each of these various types of bodies, irrespective of its title, is usually assigned some rather nebulous area of power.

Usually the picture as portrayed in the basic constitutional document varies considerably from the way in which the state is actually run. This false picture can range all the way from a totalitarian state, where the legislature and the courts described in the constitution are in actuality merely rubber stamps, to the situation where the power exercised by these bodies is reasonably similar to that assigned to them by the constitution. Many constitutions, however, are important for what they do not say rather than what they do say. For example, neither the Canadian nor the American Constitution makes any reference to political parties. In the United States a very elaborate Electoral College is established with powers defined for selecting a president. In practice this process is followed in form only; the major task, selecting the presidential candidates, is left in the hands of largely informal social groups known as political parties. Similarly, in Canada the British North America Act makes no mention of the role of the political party, even though, as in the United States, the major function of the party is to place before the electorate those persons from whom the public chooses its leaders. The British North America Act is even more mis-leading with respect to power realities than is the American constitution. This is explained by the fact that the British North America Act was in no way intended to be a comprehensive document, but rather was a formal statement in British statutory form, intended to meet the immediate political needs of assembling some of the colonies in North America into one country. Many of the dynamic and fluid political arrangements going to the core of political power were derived from Great Britain, and were effectively in operation prior to 1867 and were continued after that time. Thus the study of a constitution must not end with a study of the formal decision-making processes organized and defined by the fundamental constitutional document. For example, in Canada new and uniquely Canadian methods of solving federal problems have emerged without formal change in the positive law.

A constitution is more than a mechanical set of ground rules. It is a mirror reflecting the national soul. It reflects those values the country regards as important, and shows how these values will be protected. It is for the constitutional student to try to correlate and explain the extent to which the national idea is implemented within the day-to-day framework of political processes. Every nation's approach to these legal and political problems has much in common with that of every other nation, and much that is peculiarly the nation's own. Every nation draws, to a considerable extent, on the experience of other nations. Similarly, no state can function legally and politically without some internal recognition that it is, in at least some ways, part of a world community. Thus there have developed between states narrow legal, and wider customary, methods of communication and organization, which affect the domestic political order.

The impact of other states on a nation's internal political structure varies with size, geographical location, and material and military strength, in addition to the influence of cultural factors. In particular, the similarity in culture between France and Quebec has been a factor affecting Canada's internal constitutional structure, as reflected in Quebec's ever-growing ties with France. This relationship has been formalized and advanced by the negotiation of agreements between France and Quebec, often to the annoyance of the central Canadian government.

The time at which a nation attains what is commonly referred to as independence affects its constitutional organization. The national goals defined in a constitution are often a reflection of the preoccupations of the political leaders of the time. The preamble to the constitution of the Fourth French Republic reflects the strong counter-reaction to the almost unbridled power vested in the German occupiers who controlled France during World War II. This preamble spells out in elaborate detail that the nation, through its political framework, will strive as effectively as possible for the achievement of what are usually referred to as civil liberties or human rights. The present Japanese constitution contains a renunciation of the use of military force as a vehicle of national relations.

In many ways, however, the most remarkable of all constitutions is that of Great Britain. It is noteworthy that a powerful industrial nation with a population of fifty million can function so effectively, with so high a degree of respect for individual dignity, without the need of a basic constitutional document. This is perhaps a luxury which no other nation will ever be able to enjoy. It is a type of political arrangement which requires sagacity on the part of political participants and considerable time in which to evolve. Furthermore, it reflects a distrust of spelling out long-term social goals, and a preference for the day-by-day practical resolution of disputes.

One of the constitutional difficulties in Canada has been the instinctive desire of French-speaking Canadians for the definitive document in the grand civil law manner, as distinguished from the Anglo-Canadian pragmatic tradition in legal and political matters. The average Anglo-Canadian legal theorist usually envisages grave dangers in providing premature legal documents as a method of resolving social ills before a social consensus has emerged. French-speaking Canadians, nurtured on a civilian approach to law, prefer the grand legal design in the form of a constitution, with a maximum elucidation of details. We believe there are grave difficulties in widespread constitutional revision until some form of political consensus has emerged in Canada.

What is remarkable about the Canadian constitutional process is its very considerable adaptability to changing social and economic needs. The constitution has stood us in good stead for over a hundred years, through periods of economic depression, prosperity and two world wars. In that time there has been widespread conflict between various provinces and sections of the country and, during the depression, between socio-economic classes. Despite these hectic and turbulent times, the British North America Act, our basic constitutional document, has remained largely unchanged. Nevertheless, great changes have been made in our constitutional system, but through a gradual process of adjustment to meet new realities. The political situation since 1960 has perhaps been the most difficult of all. Many of Canada's basic institutions and constitutional arrangements have been under attack. The structure that seemed so firm in 1950 has been subjected to considerable pressure. It seemed that the strong central government at Ottawa, created during the Second World War, was to be a permanent feature of Canadian life, that the centralist spirit of the Fathers of Confederation was at last to become a permanent reality.

The death of Maurice Duplessis brought a new political era. Duplessis was a Quebec nationalist, but this meant, basically, preserving a rural and traditional French Canada. First, under the leadership of Mr. Duplessis' successor, Paul Sauvé, and later with the assumption of office of the Liberal Party under Jean Lesage and subsequent political leaders, Quebec began to assert itself as a political unit. The cry was heard that Canada was two nations. Canada's third largest federal political party, the New Democratic Party, at its founding convention, agreed that Canada was two nations. A number of writers in French

Canada began to demand that, if Canada was two nations, its political and constitutional processes would have to be adapted accordingly. It was proposed, for example, that Canada have a bi-national Senate, with equal representation for French Canada and English Canada, and a bi-national constitutional court.

Significant changes have been made in redefining the relations between the federal and provincial governments. Long before the changes demanded by Quebec, the institution known as the federal-provincial conference had emerged. This is a technique by which the federal governmental leadership sits down from time to time with pro-vincial leaders to resolve questions of federal-provincial concern. It is at these conferences that much of the future development of Canada is planned. Permanent committees emanating from these conferences have been established and are even now planning long-range financial and constitutional surveys with respect to Canada's future. This ex-tremely interesting constitutional phenomenon will be treated exten-sively, later in this work, because it is the most significant feature of recent developments in the constitutional field. In fact, the federal-provincial conference has, to some extent, replaced the Supreme Court as a vehicle for resolving jurisdictional disputes between the central and regional units in the country. In addition, since the assumption of power of the Liberal government in Quebec in 1960, there has been a significant shift of economic power away from the central government in Ottawa toward all of the provinces in general, but Quebec in particu-lar. For example, Quebec, at the time of writing, is collecting slightly over 50 percent of the income tax paid by Canadian citizens living in the province. This has been achieved by the province's withdrawal from many federal-provincial programmes, preferring to collect re-venue through a provincial system of taxation. The difficult and impor-tant question is how much autonomy for Quebec is possible, while at the same time a viable Canada is retained. It appears that a fairly high degree of decentralization is functional in Canada during times of economic prosperity. The unanswered question is whether decentrali-zation would be feasible in times of economic distress.

Canada has shown a remarkable capacity to keep nearly all of her essential constitutional structure intact. Yet, at the same time, the country's leadership, working within this framework, has been able to meet national needs. However, the stresses which the country faces at the present time are the most serious it has ever faced. The main por-tion of this work is devoted to a relatively detailed analysis of the constitutional system, which has served the country, on the whole, satisfactorily.

It is, accordingly, appropriate to begin with a few brief comments about the British North America Act of 1867. Admittedly, this statute was not intended to be a constitutional document similar to, or serving the same function as, the Constitution of the United States. It was, instead, as its name suggests, a statute of the British Parliament passed for the purpose of bringing together into one political unit some of Britain's colonies in North America. In the face of a belligerent United

States of America, which had just concluded a civil war, it seemed obvious that British North American colonial defences could be strengthened by a form of British North American union. Motivated in addition by the need for a larger economic market, the British colonists thought that economic union between them would be the beginning of a larger, more self-supporting economy. The Maritime provinces were growing increasingly conscious of their relative isolation and weakness in the North American world. Furthermore, Great Britain saw great advantages in this type of union, as it was anticipated that the colonies would become less dependent on the mother country.

Finally, and perhaps most important, the political system in the old Province of Canada had almost totally collapsed. In the period between 1841 and 1867 eighteen different ministries assumed office. The old Province of Canada, which combined what are now the provinces of Ontario and Quebec, had equal representation for the eastern and western portions in the single legislature, and an increasingly expanding English-speaking population demanded increased representation. The continual necessity of achieving a double majority — that is to say, a majority of members of both Canada East and Canada West — for every measure was becoming increasingly difficult and frustrating. To resolve their political difficulties, all the leaders of the old Province of Canada, with the exception of a small political group known as the Rouges, a left-wing radical movement in Canada East, joined together to seek with the British colonies in the Maritimes a new political union. The result of these efforts finally culminated in the passage, by the British Parliament, of the British North America Act.

This Act was in no way intended to be a definitive statement of Canada's constitutional functioning. It was assumed by the Parliament which passed it, and the Canadian politicians who inspired its birth, to be fundamentally a document stating the essential political terms necessary to bring about the union of some of the British North American colonies. The British North America Act is a completely misleading document unless read in the context of the political tradition of the men who created it. The Act, in its preamble, states that the various units desired to be "federally united into One Dominion under the Crown of the United Kingdom of Great Britain and Ireland, with a Constitution similar in Principle to that of the United Kingdom." Three significant points are made in that one tremendously significant phrase: first, the desire for some form of federal union; second, the desire to unite under the Crown of Great Britian; and third, the desire to have a constitution similar in principle to that which had evolved in the United Kingdom. It is essential, if one is to understand the Canadian constitution, to understand the deep significance of the goals expressed in that phrase. The concept of the Crown and all the legal rights and the spirit which pertain to this concept are an integral part of Canadian constituitonal life. Perhaps, however, the most important fact which must be kept in mind was the desire to develop a constitution with principles similar to those of Great Britain's. The student of Canadian government and politics must be fully cognizant of British constitutional practice, if he is to read the terms of the British North America Act intelligently. In fact, a literal reading of the Act itself is not only of little value in understanding the realities of political life, but is in fact dangerously misleading.

The Act was essentially concerned with providing for those details which the conventions and practices of British constitutionalism would not answer. For example, it was necessary to devise a method whereby the rights of the monarch could be discharged in Canada. It was necessary to set up some form of body to exercise the duty of advising the monarch's representative. It was necessary to bring into existence a legislative body for the national government. It was necessary to define the composition and powers of this legislative body. Furthermore, it was essential to re-create the old provinces of Ontario and Quebec, which had been merged into one unitary government by the Act of 1840. It was necessary to constitute the legislatures of these units and to provide for their executive government. Most important of all, it was necessary to lay down the division of powers between the federal Parliament and the provincial legislatures. Certain principles had to be sketched out with respect to the establishment of a judiciary. Some provision for Canada's treaty powers had to be made. In additon, some recognition had to be given in the statute to the positions of the English and French languages. Many sections of the Act are devoted to the detailed financial questions posed by the joining together of the colonies.

The Canadian politicians who brought about Canada's birth were content to take over from Great Britain most of the essential British constitutional principles and practices. Pragmatic in their approach to politics, they were not impressed by lofty statements of principles and goals. Though they were deeply devoted to principles of individual liberty, freedom of the judiciary and freedom from arbitrary power, they made no attempt to include in the British North America Act any grandiose statement on the rights of the individual. The rights of British citizens were, for them, sufficient. It was assumed that these rights would be enforced through the traditional methods of the common law, but, most important, through the inherent cultural tradition of respect for freedom and dissent. It was assumed that the Opposition in Parliament would be accorded its traditional freedom, and that individual citizens would be able to exercise freedom of assembly or speech. If, in any circumstance, the traditional freedoms were restrained and restricted, it was assumed that the courts would do their duty. These common law principles continue to form a major instrument in protecting the freedom of the individual. Many of the freedoms guaranteed to American citizens by the American Constitution are similarly protected in Canada, but in different ways. One of the questions that will be asked later in this book is whether the traditional methods of protecting individual liberties, without resort to a bill of rights entrenched in the constitution, is sufficient.

Despite the absence of a general statement on civil liberties in the British North American Act, there are nevertheless a number of specific rights guaranteed within its terms. First, the reference in the preamble to a constitution similar in principle to that of the United Kingdom has been referred to on occasion by Supreme Court judges in cases involving civil liberties. Furthermore, the Act recognized English and French as official languages of the country for certain purposes. They were given equal footing with respect to their use in the Parliament of Canada, in federal statutes and in the federal courts, in the Quebec courts and in the Quebec legislature. A major political question now, however, is the extent to which the French language should be officially recognized for use in the other nine provinces. Quebec has resolved the issue by making French the official language of the Province. We do not propose to deal in any detail, at the moment, with the question of civil liberties, but instead to point out that the Fathers of Confederation rather typically saw no need for grandiose or general statements on this subject.

It is also interesting to note a number of other substantial omissions from the terms of the British North America Act. No provision was made in the statute for an amendment process. The reason for this omission was, quite simply, the assumption by everyone that, since the Act had been passed by the British Parliament, it could be amended by the enacting body. Evidently the Fathers of Confederation, one of whose guiding principles was loyalty to the Crown and the British connection, saw no need for any other potential amendment process in the future. Perhaps it was not lack of foresight, but rather the desire to keep to an absolute minimum potential problems that had to be resolved at the time of Confederation. In any event, the question of amendment is another of the difficult issues facing Canadians at the present time. A whole sequence of federal-provincial conferences have been held on this question, and these will be described in fuller detail later. It is sufficient to say, however, that this has proved to be one of the toughest and most difficult of the many constitutional questions with which Canadians have had to wrestle.

It is important to note that the Act does not set up a final court of appeal for the nation. Instead, power to set up a general court of appeal is assigned to the Parliament of Canada. Once again, the assumption was made that final appeals would go to the Judicial Committee of the Privy Council sitting in London. It was probably not even considered sufficiently pressing or relevant to resolve the question of whether it was necessary to establish and provide for a final supreme court within the national boundaries. This is further evidence of the fact that the formulators of the Constitution were concerned basically with resolving the immediate problems to bring about a union of some British North American colonies. This constitutional document, as it might more appropriately be called, was a reflection of the evolutionary and pragmatic approach to politics so characteristic of the Anglo-Canadian tradition. Nothing was resolved beyond that which had to be decided immediately. Long-term political problems were not grappled with. Grandiose statements of national goals were kept to an absolute minimum. In fact, the very pragmatism which this document reflects illustrates the point made earlier, that a constitutional document mirrors the political personality of the nation. The Canadian political personality has always been one to grapple with the real issues and avoid unnecessary theoretical decisions.

The most notable omission from the Act is the failure to refer to the most important political officers within the state. At no point in the Act is any reference made to the Prime Minister. No reference is made to the Cabinet. No reference is made to political parties. No reference is made to the Leader of the Opposition. All these fundamental and important participants in the constitutional process in this country achieve their position through means other than pure reliance on the terms of the British North America Act. It must be remembered, however, that no Prime Minister, at least according to constitutional convention, may assume that office unless he is or soon becomes a member of the federal Parliament established by the B.N.A. Act. It is, however, legally possible for a Cabinet minister to hold office without being elected to Parliament. These are part of the whole host of conventions which were developed, basically in Great Britain, to control the power of the monarch and to implement the will of the electorate, and which have been adopted in Canada. To read the British North America Act would be to get a totally misleading impression of the Constitution, leading the untutored observer to conclude that the country was, in fact, ruled by the Governor General, seeking advice of the Privy Council. In reality, as a result of these customary usages, usually referred to as conventions, the political parties play the most important role in selecting a leader, who, in turn, must stand for Parliament, and who, if his party achieves a majority of seats (or, usually, a plurality — that is, more seats than any other party in Parliament), is called upon by the Governor General to form an administration. None of these rules is formulated in the positive law. Similarly, it is only convention which requires that he select members of his Cabinet from among the members of his own party in the House of Commons and in the Senate. Occasionally, however, a Cabinet minister has assumed office and then later won a seat in the legislature.

It would be unthinkable in contemporary Canada for the Governor General to exercise the many legal powers assigned to him in the British North America Act without, on almost all occasions, first obtaining the recommendations of the Prime Minister and Cabinet. For example, the power to appoint judges is vested in the Governor General. It is absolutely established that appointments to the Bench are only made upon the recommendation of the Cabinet. Furthermore, the Governor General is given a variety of other legal powers, among which are the powers of appointing members of the Senate, calling the House of Commons together, and dissolving the House. Almost all these functions are, once again, usually only exercised after a recommendation from the Prime Minister, though there have been occasions when the Governor General and his provincial counterparts, the Lieutenant-Governors, have seen fit to act on their own initiative. The general principles as to when the Governor General must act upon the advice of his chief minister, and when he has independent authority, are not determined by law but, instead, are regulated by resort to customary practices. This reflects the traditional British approach of retaining the form while subtly changing the substance of the institution, in order to have it accord with contemporary needs. It is this peculiar political device that probably more than any other is responsible for the effective, non-revolutionary approach to change that has characterized most of the English-speaking world. It creates an atmosphere where conservatives are not excessively threatened by any dramatic change in form, yet radicals are satisfied that the realities of power are being altered.

The conventions also serve to bring about the implementation of the general political will after an election. For example, the convention which, with some exceptions, requires that the Governor General choose the leader of the party with the largest number of seats in Parliament to be Prime Minister not only restricts his power of choice but also carries out the will of the electorate. However, there have been, in addition to these conventions inherited from Britain, a substantial number of distinctively Canadian conventions. For example, the effect of practice has been to nullify some of the provisions in the British North America Act. This is illustrated by looking at Section 56, which vests in the monarch the right to disallow Canadian legislation. Similarly, the B.N.A. Act provides for disallowance by the Governor General of provincial legislation. Both these legal powers have in effect, if not in law, been repealed through their failure to be used, and the unwritten political consensus is that they will probably never be used again. Certainly this is true with respect to disallowance of bills by the monarch, though there may be circumstances in which the federal power of disallowance might be used against one of the smaller provinces. Not only do we see portions of the British North America Act negatived by convention, but there are examples of traditional unwritten British parliamentary conventions actually written into the terms of the Act. For example, Section 53 provides that money bills shall originate in the lower house, Section 54 provides that money bills must be recommended to the Commons by a message from the Governor General, and Section 20 provides that there shall be a session of the Parliament of Canada at least once every year.

Furthermore, there are other aspects of law within the constitutional framework regulated by conventional practice. For example, the judiciary is subject in technical law to the will of legislators. Judicial appointment, jurisdiction and tenure are all determined by statute. It would be easy in legal theory to restrict the role and independence of the judiciary, yet convention has operated in such a way as to make the judiciary almost totally independent of political pressure. Furthermore, the civil service is by law very much at the mercy of the government, in that the tenure of the individual civil servant is in law at the pleasure of the Crown, meaning the Cabinet of the day. However, this legal power is only resorted to in cases of gross inefficiency or misconduct. By convention, the civil servant has a tenure almost equal to that of persons within the academic community, the reason for this being

11

the desire to set up a civil service selected on the basis of merit, and protected in their positions should a new administration take office. Curiously enough, it has usually been felt that the deputy minister does not enjoy this conventional protection, and his replacement by a new government composed of another party is regarded as constitutionally correct. In reality, practice seems increasingly to be protecting the deputy minister from removal.

Conventions have always played an important part in the foreign relations of Great Britain and, similarly, this is true of Canada. Though in positive law the executive has very wide powers in the area of foreign relations, it has been customary and conventional to conduct foreign policy in major areas of policy only with the support of Parliament. For example, a declaration of war or peace by the executive without the concurrence of the House of Commons, though perhaps technically lawful, would be regarded as a serious violation of constitutional practice. Furthermore, much of the development of autonomy between Canada and Great Britain has evolved through conventional arrangement. For example, technically the British North America Act is still an act of the British Parliament, yet by convention it would be unthinkable for Britain to amend that Act without the express consent of Canada. Imperial conferences and the use of political usages and conventions tended to mitigate the effect of positive law. Furthermore, it has also been a constitutional tendency in this country, in the area of relations with Great Britain, to write conventions ultimately into law. The Statute of Westminster, which essentially established the complete lawful autonomy of Canada was, in effect, a statutory enactment of practices and principles evolved over a substantial number of years. It is our contention that this is the most highly desired technique for resolving constitutional differences. In other words, once a practice has developed satisfactorily, and has generally been agreed upon by all the participants, it is then appropriate to draft a statute or other legal document embodying the political consensus.

Another area in which convention has been extremely important has been that of constitutional amendment. It is now accepted practice that provisions of the British North America Act dealing with the provinces are only amended with the consent of all of them, or with the consent of the province or provinces concerned. Furthermore, it is also practice that the federal Cabinet never requests the British Parliament to make changes in the British North America Act, except with the support of the House of Commons and the Senate.

Perhaps the most significant unwritten development in the constitutional life of the country has been the mode of working out a relationship between the federal government and the provincial governments. It is a central theme of this work that the federal-provincial or Dominion-provincial conference, whereby the leaders of provincial and federal governments sit down periodically in conference, is the most important new phenomenon in our constitutional life. In fact, it has become the practice to reach decisions at these conferences and then announce them to the federal Parliament and the provincial legislatures. Unless the legislators are willing to vote non-confidence in the Cabinet, these decisions are invariably accepted. For example, the conferences which were held on the amendment formula were held in private and agreement was reached without any consultation with either the federal Parliament or the provincial legislatures. After agreement had been reached it was possible for the legislatures only to vote approval or disapproval, but not to substantially change the terms of the agreement.

Furthermore, many disputes which were formerly resolved by the courts have now been channelled into the arena of the federal-provincial conference. The province of Quebec, for example, because of its unhappiness with the structure of the Supreme Court of Canada, has deliberately supported a policy of placing disputes within the federal-provincial conference rather than allowing their submission to the courts. Thus, two of our most important and traditional arenas of decision-making, the legislatures and the courts, have both had their traditional powers impinged upon without any formal legal change in their powers. Just as the monarch retained his powers in theory but lost them in substance to other methods of decision-making, similarly, the courts and the legislatures are in law retaining their powers, but in essence are being forced to give considerable ground to this new constitutional phenomenon, the federal-provincial conference.

Since Confederation there has been an ebb and flow of power between the central and regional governments in Canada. Recently, the federal-provincial conference has been an effective vehicle for strengthening the position of the provinces. Largely as a result of these conferences, the nation is undergoing the most profound changes in its constitutional functioning, without the vast majority of the public being fully aware of these events or their implications. Unfortunately, many of these issues are tremendously complex and technical, and do not readily catch the public interest. The whole question of very complex fiscal arrangements, such as shared cost programmes between the federal and provincial governments, does not usually excite the average newspaper reader. Yet the control of funds is usually the most important factor in the determination of power, and this is one of the major issues being resolved at federal-provincial conferences.

One of Canada's major problems is determining how much control over tax revenues can be redistributed to the provinces, while, at the same time, the federal government retains sufficient funds to maintain a viable nation. For example, as Quebec has opted out of federal cost-sharing programmes, the province has received a corresponding increase in tax revenue. The province in 1974 had achieved a situation in which over 50 per cent of the income tax paid by persons living in that province accrued to the provincial government. The Quebec government has its own hospital scheme and old age contributory pension scheme. Quebec has also suggested that the province substitute provincial schemes for the existing national programmes on family allowances, housing and unemployment insurance. Former Premier Lesage suggested that the province be allowed to collect not only the direct taxes now permitted under the constitution but also indirect taxes. Although in recent times this demand has subsided, the province has also asserted her right to conduct external negotiations with foreign countries.

A central question facing Canada's political leadership is the extent to which the Constitution should be formally altered or rewritten in order to accommodate Quebec's demands. Many Quebeckers demand that Canada draft a new constitution recognizing what they argue is the special place of Quebec in Confederation. It has been suggested by some Quebec spokesmen that the federal government should reflect the fact that Canada is composed of two linguistic groups. For example, they would contend that the judicial system of Canada should be changed so as to prohibit common law trained judges of the Supreme Court of Canada from making decisions in civil law cases coming from Quebec. In addition, opposition has been expressed by Quebec lawyers to the present arrangement whereby federal Supreme Court justices are appointed by Ottawa. It has also been suggested that some recognition should be given in the legislative branch of government to the existence of two nations, perhaps by making the Senate bi-national, so that there would be an equal number of representatives from Quebec and the rest of the country in that particular body.

Recent attempts to draft a new constitution proved to be unsuccessful. Another constitutional conference would probably provoke more disagreement than consensus. It has to be remembered that six federal-provincial attempts at finding a purely domestic formula for amending the British North America Act have all ended in failure. It would be an extremely difficult task merely to ascertain how representation would be arranged for attendance and voting at a conference on a new constitution. For example, would each province have an equal vote regardless of population? Would the central government have a voice equal to that of all the provinces? Would Quebec have a vote specially weighted in her favour? Would delegates to this constitutional convention be elected by the people, or nominated by the existing governments?

In the unlikely event that a constitutional conference reasonably satisfactory to Quebec and the rest of Canada could be called, then this body would be overwhelmed with a tremendous number of problems, including the problem of redividing legislative and fiscal jurisdiction. The conference would have to decide on who would arbitrate disputes over legislative jurisdiction between central and regional governments. It would be faced with a wide variety of demands with respect to education and language, and the role of the provincial governments in international matters would have to be resolved. The question of the monarchy and the role of the existing parliamentary system would have to be decided. These are just a few of the questions that would face further constitutional conferences attempting to draft the new constitution that is so glibly talked about and demanded.

As yet no really well argued case has been presented on why Canada needs a new constitution. Changes may be needed, but they can be made within the existing framework. It must be proved that the existing constitutional framework is so rigid that it cannot accommodate change, before Canadians should embark on drafting a new constitution. In fact, the Canadian constitution is flexible and adaptable. What is lacking in Canada is a political consensus on change, and until this is achieved a constitutional convention on a new constitution will do more harm than good.

The political tensions in Canada have resulted not only in flagrant demands for constitutional change, but also in serious reflections on many of our most important institutions. It is important that these aspersions on our institutions not go unchallenged. For example, critics of the judicial system often charge that a judge will tend to favour the government which appointed him, when faced with a dispute over federal-provincial legislative jurisdiction. There is no evidence that judges feel beholden to the government that appointed them and, in fact, a very high proportion of Supreme Court decisions have favoured the provincial position. Judges must never become arbitrators or delegates of those that appoint them. We have, throughout Anglo-Canadian legal history, striven to develop a system of judicial independence. Any attempt to destroy this tradition must be resisted. It is frightening to hear the suggestion that the Supreme Court should be composed equally of representatives from the central government and from the provinces, on the assumption that each of these appointees would render decisions in accordance with the interests of his appointing government. A suggestion of this kind destroys the fundamental assumptions upon which our judicial system is based. Some of the criticisms of the Canadian judicial court structure will be examined more fully later in this work.

It is not suggested that proposals for change be automatically resisted. Instead, it is recommended that an existing institution should be studied and understood before suggestions are made for change. There are usually reasons why an instituion is shaped the way it is, and these must be weighed and consciously discounted before an institution is abandoned or radically altered. This is the only method of social change which can provide adaptation to contemporary social needs, while retaining the best of our honourable and, on the whole, effective constitutional system.

Two

Legislative Authority

It is now appropriate to examine who has authority within the Canadian constitutional structure to make authoritative decisions. In purely legal terms, the various legislative bodies are the most formidable and important authoritative source of law in Canada. However, there are a number of bodies exercising authority delegated to them by statute, and their decisions have the same legal effect as the norms contained in a legislative enactment. This process will be examined later in this work.

Three types of legislatures have, subject to special conditions, the power to enact legislation relative to Canada: first, the Parliament of the United Kingdom, which still has certain legislative authority with respect to Canada; second, the federal Parliament, constituted, and its powers defined, by the British North America Act; third, the legislatures of the ten provinces, which have certain powers vested in them by the British North America Act and its amendments.

Before the area of authority vested in these various legislative bodies is described, it is of paramount importance to consider and explain the impact of the concept of the supremacy of Parliament. This concept has had an immense effect on the evolution of Canada's constitutional structure. The principle was inherited from the Constitution of Great Britain, and continues to play a fundamental role in defining constitutional arrangements in Canada. What does the doctrine mean? An examination of the supremacy doctrine in the United Kingdom facilitates explanation. In that country it means that, to the judiciary, the power of Parliament is unlimited. In other words, Parliament can make any law it wishes, or repeal any law that it wishes. It means, in essence, that the courts have no authority to declare illegal any statute passed by Parliament. It means that no Parliament is bound by an act of its predecessors, consequently giving every Parliament the right to change or undo the obligations established by preceding Parliaments.

Stated in this bald way, the doctrine is very frightening, because, carried to its logical conclusion, it means that Parliament could obliterate the Opposition, restrict freedom of speech, deny traditional procedures before the courts, or even abolish the courts themselves. It is, however, important to recognize that there are a variety of cultural, psychological and political implications which mitigate against the use by Parliament of its incredible power. First, the courts have utilized their role as interpreters of legislation to mitigate the effects of certain types of legislation. The courts, because of the doctrine of parliamentary supremacy, will not state that a statute is unconstitutional, but will instead pay lip service to its legality. The cardinal rule of judicial interpretation developed by English judges is that they attempt to find the intent of Parliament as expressed by the plain meaning of the words within the four corners of the Act. It is, however, most unlikely that a case would be before the courts if the words of the statute were unambiguous and the intent of Parliament absolutely clear. In their purported search for the intent of the legislature, the courts have developed a set of statutory rules for judicial interpretation, which include a whole body of presumptions which Parliament is assumed to have had in mind when passing the act. For example, it is presumed that Parliament never intends to deny a subject access to the courts. The courts will state that, in the absence of very clear and unequivocal language in the statute, they will not interpret a statute in such a way as to deprive a subject of this right. Furthermore, the courts will presume that, in the absence of express words in the statute, it will be assumed that it is not to have retrospective effect. They will presume that there is to be no interference with vested rights, or substantial alteration of the law, unless the words of the statute are very clear. They will presume that in criminal cases *mens rea*, the concept which requires foreseeability on the part of an accused, is a required part of every offence, unless it is clearly intended to be excluded by the statute. These rules of statutory interpretation, of which the foregoing are only a small sample, have tended to produce what is often referred to as a common law bill of rights. It is, however, important not to over-estimate the effect of judicial interpretation, because it is only in the event of lack of clarity in the wording of the act that the courts can resort to these techniques of interpretation to bring about what they regard as a just result. The concept of parliamentary supremacy involves the notion that, if the words of the act are clear, they must be given full effect.

It is, accordingly, in defining the relationship between the courts and Parliament that the doctrine has been most significant. It has meant that British courts have never assumed the very powerful role of the American judiciary. In the United States the judges, in effect, are the ultimate expositors of community values through their role as interpreters of the federal and state constitutions. In the American system the courts are able to declare any legislation unconstitutional on the ground that it violates the terms of the United States or state constitutions, depending on the circumstances. Using this power of judicial review, the courts have ruled unconstitutional a substantial amount of attempted legislation. In fact, the United States Supreme Court's role has become a very aggressive one, as is demonstrated by the decision that the states must undertake reapportionment of legislative districts to accord with the principles of voting equality. The English constitutionalist would find the proposition that a court could reorganize, through judicial order, the system of legislative districts incredible. This is a matter which, in British constitutional practice, is left to the legislatures, and any attempt at intervention by the courts would be regarded as improper and unconstitutional by all participants in the British political process.

One of the most significant effects of the doctrine of parliamentary supremacy has been its psychological impact on the judiciary. British judges have for so long regarded the concept of parliamentary supremacy as binding, that they have often tended to become mechanical in their approach to legislation, as well as somewhat timid in the exercise of the judicial function. In defence of the concept of parliamentary supremacy and the less aggressive role of the courts, it is the parliamentarians who are elected by the populace, and who are ultimately directly accountable to their constituents. Though judicial activism is now popular with many professional law teachers and political scientists, among others, these same classes of persons in the United States once decried, especially in the 1920's and early 1930's, judicial intervention which rendered many acts of Congress unconstitutional. At that time, judges in the United States played a powerful role in frustrating the social aims of many American statutes, much to the consternation of many American liberals. Thus, the use of judicial power in the United States provides satisfaction or frustration, largely depending upon the observer's objectives. There are valid grounds for concern in the United States about the excessive exercise of a policy-making role by men who are appointed by the executive and virtually accountable to no one. It is not the decisions they render that are excessively frightening, but rather the fact that the courts have had to step into areas which, in our view, rightly belong to the legislature. There does, however, seem to be a lack of confidence, on the part of many informed Americans, in the legislative process, particularly at the state level. These people would argue that the wide use of judicial power is a most welcome method of preventing legislative faults, and providing initiative where legislators will not act.

In support of the doctrine of legislative supremacy as found in Great Britain, one can argue that it allows the legislature to act, unhampered by judicial veto, in the manner which it regards as most beneficial to the public interest. In addition, since the Cabinet only remains in power if it has the support of a majority of that body, there is nothing to stop a vigorous administration from dealing immediately and effectively with the social and other ills through the use of legislative action. Proponents of judicial review would argue that this is a frightening state of affairs, in that some ultimate check should be placed upon an administration which, perhaps, might use Parliament as a rubber stamp in order to achieve its ends. The supporters of the

British system would probably argue that public opinion and the need to win elections provides all the restraint necessary. Perhaps the most significant point to remember is that different countries need different methods of approach. It is unwise to baldly compare a constitutional rule in one country with that of another, and come to any definite conclusions, without a full explanation of the constitutional and political differences in the two countries. Certainly, as far as Great Britain is concerned, parliamentary supremacy has not resulted in any excessive abuse of power. Similarly, in the United States, judicial review has proved of great benefit, particularly in recent years, in preventing intrusions upon civil liberties.

Legislative supremacy was established in Great Britain as a result of the struggle between the House of Commons and the monarch. The common law lawyers, who were the allies of the Commons in this struggle with the Crown, conceded the dominance of the legislature. This was done in order to counteract the claim of the king that he could rule by virtue of his prerogative power, and this has meant that many of Britain's important constitutional documents are only in ordinary statutory form. Under the doctrine of parliamentary supremacy any of these statutes can be changed at any time by any Parliament. It is an essential ingredient of the concept of parliamentary supremacy that Parliament cannot bind itself. Thus, it is argued that since Parliament is supreme, nothing that went on before can restrict the legislative power of the existing Parliament. It is, however, well known that there are a variety of restraints above and beyond those defined within the rules of the legal system in its most technical sense. Perhaps in many respects the non-legal restraints on the use of power are the most important. In fact, to a community determined to destroy its freedom of speech, freedom of assembly, and other important rights, it is unlikely that any statement on a piece of paper is going to deter the pursuit of that objective. Thus, civil liberties have been protected as well in Great Britain as in any country in the world, despite the development of the notion of parliamentary supremacy.

It is now possible to examine the Canadian constitutional system and analyze the impact of the doctrine of the supremacy of Parliament. The preamble to the British North America Act provided that Canada was to have "a Constitution similar in Principle to that of the United Kingdom." Since the most important principle of British constitutional law is the supremacy of Parliament, we must conclude that it is part of our constitutional system. This, however, is not merely a conjecture, but has received judicial approval in a number of cases, the most important of which will be discussed later. The major difficulty, however, in the Canadian system as it relates to parliamentary supremacy is the fact that legislative power in Canada has been divided primarily between the federal Parliament and the provincial legislatures. To complicate the matter, however, there are certain enactments of the British Parliament which still have validity in relation to Canada, the most important, of course, being the British North America Act and its amendments. The question is, therefore, how has the concept of parliamentary supremacy been reconciled with the fact that three legislatures have authority to pass statutes within the Canadian constitutional framework?

The statutory authority of the United Kingdom Parliament results from the fact that, in order to bring together the three British colonies of Canada, New Brunswick and Nova Scotia, it was necessary to enact the legislation in the British Parliament. This legislation, entitled The British North America Act, 1867,[1] was, as outlined earlier in this book, largely the result of Canadian effort, yet the formal enactment was done by the Imperial Parliament. This document is still the most important one relating to the constitutional process in Canada. The Act has been amended upon a number of occasions, usually by the British Parliament itself. There have, however, been amendments to the statute by the federal Parliament and by the provincial legislatures. There are a number of sections of the Act which specifically provide that they are only to exist until the Parliament of Canada otherwise provides. Sections 35, 40, 41 and 47 are all illustrations of the federal Parliament's ability to make changes without recourse to British parliamentary action. Similarly, some sections of the Act provide that they are to remain in existence until "the Legislature of Quebec (or Ontario) otherwise provides." Sections 78, 83 and 84 are examples of provisions of this kind. In addition, Section 92 (1) provides that the legislature of the province has the right to amend the provincial constitution "except as regards the Office of Lieutenant-Governor." Under this grant of power the legislatures of Ontario and Quebec have changed the terms of Section 85 to allow a legislature to run for five years, rather than the previous limit of four years as stated in the section.

The most significant development, however, with respect to amendment of the British North America Act was the passage, in 1949, of the British North America Act, 1949 (No. 2).[2] This amendment to the constitution passed by the British Parliament became incorporated in the original body of the Act as Section 91 (1). It is this amendment to the statute that transfers to the federal Parliament the right to change any portion of the statute except a listed number of powers outlined in Section 91 (1). Any change with respect to sections of the Act dealing with these classes of subjects still requires legislative action by the British Parliament. These powers included those sections of the Act dealing with schools, the use of the English and French language, the requirement that there be a session of the Canadian Parliament at least once a year, and that no House of Commons continue for more than five years. Furthermore, and undoubtedly the most important sections of the British North America Act not amendable by the federal Parliament alone, are those sections of the Act concerned with classes of subjects, rights and privileges belonging to provincial legislatures. Thus, although this amendment to the British North America Act transfers to the federal Parliament substantial power to amend the Act, nevertheless, the amendment reserves for exclusive British parliamentary action some of the most important sections of the statute. The reasons for this are, of course, quite clear, in that in any federal system it is generally regarded as undesirable to vest in either the federal legislature or the provincial legislatures unilateral control over the legislative authority of the other legislature or legislatures exercising power under the constitution. It has meant that, in order to change substantial portions of Canada's basic constitutional document, resort must be had to the British Parliament. This has been a cause of considerable concern to many Canadians, not on the grounds of inconvenience or technical difficulty, but rather on the nationalist argument that this is inconsistent with a true national sovereignty. Later in this work the most recent and unsuccessful proposals to develop an amendment process which does not require resort to the British Parliament are outlined. Nevertheless, at the time of writing, at least in formal statutory terms, the United Kingdom Parliament is still a source of positive law in Canada. It is, of course, important to note that the United Kingdom Parliament will not act except at the request of the Canadian federal government, yet many contend that this is embarrassing to Canada. A much more substantial objection to this process is the possibility that the federal Parliament might seek an amendment to the Constitution, to which some, or all, of the provinces might be opposed. This would place the British Parliament in a most awkward and embarrassing situation, though the general practice has been for this Parliament to acknowledge communications only from the federal government, on the ground that only it speaks for the entire country.

The British North America Act, since 1867, has been amended on a number of occasions, most of the amendments being of a relatively minor nature. There have, however, been some of prime importance, such as the one just mentioned, namely the British North America Act, 1949, (No. 2), the 1940 amendment,[3] which vests jurisdiction over unemployment insurance with the federal Parliament, the 1951 amendment,[4] which gives the federal Parliament shared authority over old age pensions with the provincial legislatures, the 1960 amendment, dealing with the tenure of office of judges,[5] and the 1965 amendment dealing with the tenure of Senators.[6]

Besides the British North America Act and its amendments, however, there are other United Kingdom statutes applicable to Canada, the most important of which is the Statute of Westminster, 1931.[7] It is this statute which gives full positive legal recognition to the proposition established by convention and at Imperial conferences that the British Parliament will not legislate for Canada, except with the consent and at the request of the Canadian federal government. Furthermore, it is provided that no Canadian statute will be void or inoperative on the ground that it is inconsistent with any British statute. Furthermore, Section 2(2) of the Act gives the Canadian Parliament the power to repeal any British statute, order, rule or regulation, "insofar as the same is part of the Law of the Dominion." It was necessary, however, to place in the Statute of Westminster a provision (Section 7) to the effect that "Nothing in this Act shall be deemed to apply to the repeal, amendment or alteration of the British North America Acts, 1867 to 1930, or any order, rule or regulation made thereunder." The reason for the inclusion of this section was the fear on the part of the provinces that by virtue of the Statute of Westminster the Canadian Parliament would be able to unilaterally amend any portion of the British North America Act. This would mean that, without going to Britain or consulting the provinces, Parliament would have legal power to alter the division of legislative power outlined in the British North America Act. The provinces have regarded the necessity for United Kingdom legislative action as a protection of their legislative rights.

It is now appropriate to examine legislative authority in Canada, and to examine this power in the light of the principle of the supremacy of Parliament. The overriding question is the extent to which the doctrine of parliamentary supremacy which evolved in Britain with its unitary system of government, has operated in and affected the Canadian constitutional system. Prior, however, to analysing this question, it is necessary to examine briefly parliamentary power and functioning.

Canada's Parliament was created, and its powers defined, by the British North America Act. Section 17 provides that Parliament will consist of "the Queen, an Upper House styled the Senate, and the House of Commons." The most important element of the three is the House of Commons which, at the time of writing, consists of 264 elected members.[8] There are a number of other provisions in the British North America Act dealing with the conduct of the House of Commons; however, it is not necessary to examine them at present. The composition of the Senate of Canada is also defined by various sections of the Act. For example, the body has a membership of 102 persons.[9] Unlike the American Senate, which has two senators from each state, the Canadian Senate has a certain number of senators from various divisions within the nation. Ontario, Quebec, the Western Provinces, and the Maritime Provinces are entitled to 24 senators, and Newfoundland to 6. The members of the Senate are appointed by the Governor General under the terms of Section 24 of the Act. By convention, however, they are named only after a recommendation from the Prime Minister. The functions of the Queen are carried out by her representative in Canada, the Governor General.

In order for a bill to become a statute, it must be approved by all the constituent elements of the Parliament of Canada. In effect, however, this means approval by the House of Commons, as the tendency has been for the Governor General, and to a large extent the Senate, to act as rubber stamps for the action of the House. The House of Commons is essentially controlled by the Prime Minister and his Cabinet who, by constitutional custom, must ultimately obtain seats in the House of Commons or the Senate. It is unusual to have more than one member of the Cabinet chosen from the Senate. The general tendency has been for the Cabinet to exercise overwhelming influence in the House of Commons, and there is considerable fear that the House of Commons itself is acting as a formal stamp, largely at the whim of the Cabinet. For a considerable part of the twentieth century, the tendency in Canadian politics was for one party to have a substantial majority in the House of Commons. In recent years, however, there have been several governments which did not command an over-all majority of the members in the House of Commons. The existence of minority government has added considerable life to the day-to-day activity of the House.

The Cabinet exercises a stranglehold over the legislative process in that only members of the Cabinet have authority to introduce bills which require the expenditure of funds. Furthermore, the private member is handicapped not only in that he cannot introduce money bills, but also by the fact that only a small portion of House time is devoted to consideration of private members' bills. This usually means that private members' bills are never voted upon and are returned to the bottom of the parliamentary order paper. The conduct of business within the House of Commons is determined and controlled by the Cabinet of the day. It is, however, Canadian practice for members of each political party in the House to gather together privately in what is referred to as caucus. During the course of these gatherings there is an opportunity for the ordinary member of Parliament who belongs to the Government party to voice his disapproval of Government policy. The members of the Government party are at least theoretically equal in caucus, and therefore Cabinet members must present some defence of Government policy to the party back-benchers. As sessions of the caucus are conducted in private, it is difficult for the outsider to judge the effectiveness of private member influence over Cabinet members as a result of these gatherings.

An affirmative vote in the Senate is required for all bills passed by the House of Commons before they can be enacted into law. This in theory gives the Senate tremendous legal power, but, like so much purely legal power, it is exercised subject to political considerations. The function of the Senate has been largely to act as a board of review, tidying up Commons legislation and carrying out some important committee functions. Essentially, however, the Senate has never seen fit to really use its tremendous legal power, and it is unlikely to do so. It is interesting to note that the Constitution provides, in Section 26, that the Queen, upon the recommendation of the Governor General, may add four to eight members to the Senate. This provision was included in the statute in order to allow for the breaking of a deadlock between the Commons and the Senate, should one occur. It is also interesting to note that these appointments are left to the Queen but, by convention, would be made only upon the advice of the government of the day. The Canadian Senate has been the object of considerable criticism, and even ridicule, but it is not appropriate at this moment to analyse these criticisms or answer them.[10]

There are, within the terms of the British North America Act, a number of sections dealing with the organization and functioning of both the Senate and House of Commons, including such important sections as those dealing with the length of time a House of Commons shall continue in existence without an election — five years[11] — and the fact that there shall be a session of Parliament at least once in every year.[12] We do not propose to delve into the details of the functioning of the parliamentary process in this work, but rather to analyse briefly the legal effectiveness of parliamentary action.

For the former colonies of Nova Scotia and New Brunswick, the British North America Act continued their existing legislatures.[13] With respect to Ontario and Quebec, however, since they were not separate legal units prior to 1867, it was necessary to create a new legislature for each province. Section 69 created a legislature for Ontario, consisting of the Legislative Assembly and the Lieutenant-Governor. Section 71 of the Act created a legislature for Quebec consisting of a Lieutenant-Governor and a lower and upper house. (The Quebec legislature passed an Act in December 1968, abolishing the upper house and re-naming the Legislative Assembly the National Assembly.)[14] In various other sections — 73 to 80, among others — the Act provided for the constitutional functioning of these two newly created legislatures. Nevertheless, it must be remembered that Section 92 (1) of the Act allows the legislature of each province to change its constitution in any way it sees fit, except with respect to the office of Lieutenant-Governor. The legislatures of the remaining provinces were constituted in a variety of ways. British Columbia was admitted to Confederation in 1871 by virtue of an order-in-council passed by the British Privy Council under authority delegated to it by Section 146 of the British North America Act, 1867. It was provided in this order-in-council (Section 14 of the Schedule) that the legislature of the province would continue in existence, subject to any later changes made under the authority of the British North America Act. Similarly, an order-in-council of the British Privy Council, under the same section of the Act, continued the constitution and functioning of the legislature of Prince Edward Island, subject again to any later changes made in its functioning as authorized by the British North America Act. The province of Manitoba was created by a federal statute[15] that also provided a basic constitution for the province. Section 9 of the Act provided for a legislature consisting of the Lieutenant-Governor and two houses, subsequently reduced to one with the abolition of the upper house in 1876. Similarly, both the provinces of Alberta and Saskatchewan were created and had their constitutional structure defined by two statutes passed by the federal Parliament. The Alberta Act of 1905[16] provided, in Section 12, that there should be a legislature consisting of the Lieutenant-Governor and a Legislative Assembly. The Saskatchewan Act of 1905[17] provided for the establishment of an identical legislature in Saskatchewan. Newfoundland was made a part of Canada by British parliamentary action in the form of the British North America Act, 1949, (No. 1).[18]

It is now appropriate, after some of the legal complexities involved in creating the federal Parliament and the various provincial legislatures have been analysed, to examine the type of authority vested in the provincial legislatures as opposed to that given to the federal Parliament. In this examination it is important to remember the description of the power still vested in the British Parliament with respect to Canada. The question of to what extent the doctrine of the supremacy of Parliament is carried through into the Canadian constitutional system now arises.

Legislative power in Canada is divided between the federal Parliament and the provincial legislatures under the terms of Sections 91, 92, 93, 94, 94(A), 95, 101 and 132 of the British North America Act. These sections and their judicial interpretation have been commented on in great detail by many writers. It is, accordingly, very difficult to add anything to what has already been said about the meaning of the words in the statute which distributed legislative power. The general thrust of commentary has been to the effect that the Fathers of Confederation intended that residual power and the most important legislative responsibilities should be vested in the federal Parliament. It is our view that this interpretation is correct, as the words in the statute seem to point clearly to the conclusion that the federal Parliament was to be predominant with respect to legislative responsibility.

Section 91, which is the most important section with respect to defining the jurisdiction of the federal Parliament, vests in that body the authority to "make Laws for the Peace, Order and good Government of Canada." In addition the first portion of Section 91 provides that "for greater Certainty, but not so as to restrict the Generality of the foregoing Terms of this Section, it is hereby declared that (notwithstanding anything in this Act) the exclusive Legislative Authority of the Parliament of Canada extends to all Matters coming within the Classes of Subjects next herein-after enumerated; that is to say. . . ." There then follows a list, originally comprising twenty-nine, and now thirty-one, specific subsections giving examples of areas in which the federal Parliament has jurisdiction. An examination of the sections indicates that most of what were considered matters of particular importance in 1867 were given to the federal Parliament. It is particularly interesting to note how many of these examples of the general power given to the federal Parliament deal with matters relating to commerce. For example, various subsections give the federal Parliament control over savings banks, weights and measures, interest, legal tender, bankruptcy and insolvency, patents of invention and discovery, and copyrights in addition to a very general subsection vesting in the federal Parliament the regulation of trade and commerce. Because the Act was drafted at a time when private enterprise functioned with a minimum of governmental intervention, and the leaders of the commercial community were the most influential in the nation, it no doubt reflected their desire that this area should come within Parliament's sphere. In addition, these general commercial powers were probably placed with the federal Parliament to ease the fears of the English-speaking business community of Montreal about the possibilities of their commercial activities being rendered subject to the control of a French-Canadian-dominated provincial legislature. Thus, it would seem from the reading of Section 91 that residual powers — that is to say any legislative powers not specifically assigned by the terms of the Act — were to rest with the federal Parliament. There is further evidence provided by the enumerated powers in Section 91 of the thesis that the chief political personalities who brought Canada into being intended to vest in the federal government most matters of national importance: for example, the fact that the federal Parliament is given authority to raise money by "any Mode or System of Taxation." This power can probably be viewed in conjunction with the aforementioned authority over matters of commerce. Obviously, political authority is largely dependent on control of money and commerce and, therefore, these matters were placed within the federal parliamentary sphere.

Though a large proportion of the subsections of Section 91 deal with commercial and economic matters, a number of other subjects, which were of considerable importance both in 1867 and at the present time, are spelled out. Examples of these are: 91 (5) "Postal Service," 91 (10) "Navigation and Shipping," 91 (12) "Sea Coast and Inland Fisheries," 91 (13) "Ferries between a Province and any British or Foreign Country or between Two Provinces," 91 (24) "Indians and Lands reserved for the Indians," 91 (25) "Naturalization and Aliens," and 91 (27) "The Criminal Law, including matters of Criminal Procedure." The inclusion of this last power within the federal ambit is extremely important, as it recognizes the need for uniform standards in this area. In the United States, the vesting of this power over criminal law in the individual states was, in our view, a mistake. It has resulted in cases of men being judged criminals in one state yet not considered so in another. Furthermore, it is interesting to note that in Section 92 (10) the federal Parliament is given other jurisdictional authority. This subsection of Section 92 vests "Local Works and Undertakings" within the provincial sphere, except "Railways, Canals, Telegraphs and other Works" between provinces or extending beyond provincial limits which, along with the regulation of steamships travelling between the province and any British or foreign country, are placed under federal legislative control. Especially noteworthy is Section 92 (10) (c) which allows the federal Parliament to declare any "Works" to be for the general advantage of Canada and thereby within federal jurisdiction. Even if the "Works" is wholly situated within one province, it can be declared under the terms of this section subject to the jurisdiction of the federal Parliament. Presumably the word "Works" is to be read in conjunction with the previous words, namely "Railways, Canals, Telegraphs" and steamships and it is, accordingly, indicative of the intention of the Fathers of Confederation to place ultimate control over transportation and other forms of communication within federal authority.

Section 92 of the Act outlines most of the provincial legislative authority. The general words of this section are very brief compared with those in Section 91. Furthermore, the words at the beginning of Section 92 provide that the province "may exclusively make Laws in relation to Matters coming within the Classes of Subjects next hereinafter enumerated." This certainly supports the proposition that residual power was to rest with the federal Parliament, whereas the provincial legislatures were to be confined to the subject matters defined in the sixteen subsections of Section 92 and other relevant sections of the Act.

There are a number of general comments that can be made on these subsections. First, the assigned powers are of a relatively limited nature. Secondly, in a large number of these subsections it is specifically provided that the power is only to be exercised for the carrying out of a provincial or local purpose. For example, the provincial legislatures are given authority to impose direct taxation, but it must be for "the raising of a Revenue for Provincial Purposes." Similarly, subsection 92 (9) gives the right to raise revenue by virtue of "Shop, Saloon, Tavern, Auctioneer, and other Licences," but only for "the raising of a Revenue for Provincial, Local, or Municipal Purposes." Furthermore, the power to incorporate companies has the limitation that these corporations must have "Provincial Objects" (92 (11)). The most important powers given to the provincial legislatures, in our view, are the authority over "Public Lands belonging to the Province" (92 (5)), the control over "Local Works and Undertakings" (92 (10)) (though here it must be remembered the exceptions to this subsection are vested in the federal sphere), "Property and Civil Rights in the Province" (92 (13)), and the "Administration of Provincial Justice," including the organization and establishment of the judicial hierarchy (92 (14)). The provincial legislatures are also given authority to impose sanctions in order to enforce provincial legislation (92 (15)).

Section 92 (16) vests a small residual power in the legislatures of the provinces. It provides that they have power to legislate on "all Matters of a merely local or private Nature in the Province." It is unlikely that this was meant to vest in the provincial legislatures any wide degree of authority. Through judicial interpretation Subsection 92 (13), "Property and Civil Rights in the Province," has become the main basis for provincial legislative authority. It is quite likely that this subsection was originally intended only to vest in the provinces control over private law matters, such as contract, tort, property, wills, and mortgages. Since the Quebec Act of 1774, Quebec has had, by right, its own system of civil law, based on the European civil law tradition. It is our view that the term "Property and Civil Rights" was intended to continue Quebec's authority in this area. This interpretation is further supported by reading Section 94 of the Act, which allows for uniformity, by virtue of federal legislation, for Ontario, Nova Scotia, and New Brunswick with respect to "Property and Civil Rights," in those provinces, if they wish to delegate authority over this field to the federal Parliament. Thus, if one reads the term "Property and Civil Rights," in 92 (13), in relation to its meaning in Section 94, it seems fairly clear that all that was intended by this phrase was the traditional area known as private law which means, largely, those legal principles which determine the relationships between private citizens.

In summary, a reading of Sections 91 and 92 leads one to the conclusion that the Act vests in the federal Parliament general authority for making laws over Canada, with the exception of sixteen specific areas which have been assigned to the provincial legislatures. The draftsmen of the Act — fortunately or unfortunately, depending on one's point of view — enumerated a number of examples of the general power vested in the federal Parliament and, as we shall later see, the trend of judicial reasoning has been to weigh the heads of power in Section 91 against those in Section 92, with a resultant tendency, except in emergencies, to ignore the general grant of power in Section 91. Since the Second World War, however, the Judicial Committee of the Privy Council and the Supreme Court of Canada have in several decisions given recognition to the "Peace, Order and good Government" clause as a source of federal legislative authority in other than emergency situations.[19]

Section 93 of the Act provides that in each province "the Legislature may exclusively make Laws in relation to Education." This authority, however, is subject to a certain number of restrictions outlined in the section. A province cannot prejudicially affect rights and privileges that had been accorded to denominational schools at the time of union. Furthermore, wherever a province has a separate school system, or one is subsequently established by provincial legislation, the members of the separate school system have the right to appeal to the Governor-General-in-Council any action or decision of a provincial authority which affects the Protestant and Roman Catholic educational rights that either existed at the time of union or were thereafter established by legislation. If an appeal establishes a violation of these rights the Governor-General-in-Council is authorized to make recommendations concerning steps necessary to protect the educational rights of these religious groups.

In the event that the province does not take appropriate action, the Parliament of Canada is given legislative authority in subsection 93 (4) to "make remedial Laws for the due Execution of the Provisions of this Section and of any Decision of the Governor-General-in-Council under this Section." This interesting provision was included mainly owing to the urging of Alexander Galt, the chief spokesman of the English-speaking Protestant minority of Quebec. This group was frightened about having their educational system exclusively under the authority of the Quebec legislature, the majority of whose members were French-speaking and Roman Catholic.

The supervisory jurisdiction over education vested in the central government is further evidence of the strongly centralist nature of the British North America Act. This supervisory power in Section 93 is somewhat similar to the power vested in the Governor-General-in-Council to disallow any provincial legislation. The special supervisory powers in Section 93 were probably meant to supplement the disallowance power in a very special field, as the section allows the federal government power to cover the situation where a change was made in educational rights by a method other than resort to legislative action. It should be noted that Section 93 (3) provides that an appeal lies to the Governor-General-in-Council for any "Act or Decision." This means that there is a right of appeal from a purely administrative action, whereas the disallowance power vested in the Governor-General-in-Council can only be utilized if the province takes the formal step of passing a statutory enactment in order to change existing rights. Recently, in Quebec, a change was made in the apportionment of tax revenues as between the Catholic and Protestant school systems. The Protestant School Board of Montreal briefly contemplated the possibility of an appeal to the federal Cabinet under the terms of Section 93, but finally decided against this course of action. This reflects the trend whereby central government control mechanisms, such as disallowance, reservation, and appeals under Section 93, are very rarely used. [20]

Reference has already been made to Section 94, which outlines a scheme whereby there can be a uniform federal statute relating to laws on property and civil rights and civil procedure in Ontario, Nova Scotia and New Brunswick. This section has never been used, but once again demonstrates the strong centralist tendencies evidenced throughout the British North America Act. It is, however, significant to note that Quebec is not mentioned in Section 94 as being one of those provinces which can be part of a scheme for uniformity in the area of property and civil rights.

Section 94A is one of four amendments to the British North America Act which affected the distribution of legislative power. First, a 1940 amendment [21] vests unemployment insurance within the federal legislative sphere. This was necessary because of an earlier judicial decision which had declared federal legislation in this field to be an encroachment on the area reserved for the provinces. Section 91 (1) dealt with the federal Parliament's power to amend the British North America Act, 1867. [22] Section 94A was added to the British North America Act by virtue of an amendment in 1951, [23] and was subsequently amended in 1964. [24] This section now declares that the Canadian Parliament has authority to make laws in relation to old age pensions and supplementary benefits. It is interesting, however, that it also provides that any federal enactment in this field will not affect either existing or future provincial legislation with respect to this subject. This provision for provincial paramountcy in the event of a clash is a departure from the general scheme of both the statute and the trend of judicial decisions. Both these sources almost invariably provide for federal supremacy in the event of a clash when both federal and provincial legislatures are within a justifiable sphere of activity. This is evidenced by the next section of the Act providing for the division of legislative authority.

Section 95 provides that agriculture and immigration are areas in which the Parliament of Canada and the provinces may legislate. It is specifically provided that in the event of a legislative clash federal legislation is to prevail. Probably the significant reason why the rule with respect to paramountcy varies is that Section 95 was placed in the original Act at a time when the federal government was intended to be dominant, whereas 94A was made a part of the Act at a time when a combination of judicial decisions and political events had increased the role of the provinces beyond that intended and envisaged at the time of Confederation.

Section 132 provides that the Parliament of Canada "shall have all Powers necessary or proper for performing the Obligations of Canada or of any Province thereof, as Part of the British Empire, towards

Foreign Countries, arising under Treaties between the Empire and such Foreign Countries." This, in effect, means that when Canada was a party to an Empire treaty, it had jurisdiction to implement, through legislation, the treaty obligations of the nation. Thus, if a treaty dealt with an area normally within provincial jurisdiction, the federal Parliament nevertheless had authority to implement it by statute. Since the Empire treaty is now obsolete, and the courts have chosen to interpret the section literally, it is seemingly dead as a source of legislative authority.

The foregoing analysis of the sections dividing legislative powers lends strong support to those who argue that the Fathers of Confederation, led by Sir John A. Macdonald, desired that the central government should be very powerful and should essentially dominate the new nation. In summary, the following indications of this objective should be recalled. The residual power is vested in the federal Parliament. The federal Parliament may declare a work to the general advantage of Canada, and thereby assume jurisdiction. The federal Parliament may intervene, under certain circumstances, as regards to education. Although joint jurisdiction is given over agriculture and immigration, federal enactments are to prevail in the event of a clash. Only Section 94A, a relatively recent amendment to the statute, reflects any tendency toward predominance of provincial legislative power over federal authority.

There is now, however, little utility in pointing out that the British North America Act was designed to provide strong federal parliamentary and executive authority; it is more important to understand the evolution of the constitution in terms of political realities. These trends will be discussed in the following sections of this work. In particular, the significant impact on constitutional development of both judicial interpretation of the British North America Act, and, more lately, the impact of decisions emanating from federal-provincial conferences will be noted. The ineffectiveness of these centralizing clauses in the British North America Act serves as a classic example of the futility of written positive law in the face of a social environment which refuses to accept the original statutory intention.

It is now appropriate to analyse what is perhaps the most significant concept in Canadian constitutional law, namely the supremacy of Parliament. The doctrine has already been outlined in relation to Great Britain, but what has been its impact in Canada? It is the most important concept in determining the relationship between the courts and the federal and provincial legislatures. Recognition of this doctrine has militated against the development of a system of judicial review similar to that which exists in the United States, though the courts have retained the right of striking down legislation on the ground that the subject does not fall within the appropriate federal or provincial legislative power. Presumably the doctrine of the supremacy of Parliament is an inheritance from the British system, at least partly as a result of the general statement in the preamble to the British North America Act of a desire to establish "a Constitution similar in Principle to that of the United Kingdom."

The doctrine has received judicial support in Canada, both with respect to the provincial legislatures and the federal Parliament. The leading decision on the subject is *Hodge v. The Queen*.[25] In that case the appellant, Archibald G. Hodge, contended that his conviction for a violation of a regulation made by the Board of Licence Commissioners for the City of Toronto, acting under authority delegated to them by provincial legislative enactment, was invalid. He argued, first, that the statute was outside the scope of provincial legislative power and, secondly, that if it was within provincial legislative power the province did not have the constitutional right to delegate this authority to a regulatory body. The appellant attempted unsuccessfully to contend that the Ontario provincial legislature was essentially a creature of the Imperial Parliament and therefore had no authority to re-delegate powers assigned to it. This argument was based on the maxim, *delegatus non potest delegare*, which means in essence that a delegate cannot re-delegate. It is our view that this is merely a maxim of statutory interpretation and is not a rule of law. The Privy Council held that the provincial legislatures were in no way delegates of the Imperial Parliament, or acting under their authority. In fact, the Judicial Committee went on to say that the provincial legislature had "authority as plenary and as ample within the limits prescribed by Section 92 as the Imperial Parliament in the plenitude of its power possessed and could bestow. Within these limits of subjects and area the local legislature is supreme and has the same authority as the Imperial Parliament, or the Parliament of the Dominion would have had under like circumstances, to confide to a municipal institution, or body of its own creation, authority to make by-laws or resolutions as to subjects specified in the enactment. . . ." This meant that the provincial legislatures were, in carrying out the exercise of their legislative responsibilities under Section 92, little Imperial Parliaments; that is to say, they had the full authority to delegate any of their assigned legislative powers to any body of their choice. But, more important, this was a directive to the courts that, once they had found a subject to be within the provincial legislative sphere, as defined by the British North America Act, the will of the legislature was to prevail. The importance of this decision cannot be overemphasized in the development of constitutional government in Canada. Not only was it very significant legally, but it was also extremely important psychologically in underlining the importance of the provincial legislative role in Canada's constitutional structure.

The doctrine received judicial approval, with respect to the federal Parliament, in the Privy Council decision in the case of *British Coal Corporation v. The King*.[26] This case dealt with the question of whether the Parliament of Canada was justified in abolishing criminal appeals from the Supreme Court of Canada and the Courts of Appeal of the provinces to the Judicial Committee of the Privy Council. In a previous decision, *Naden v. The King*,[27] the Privy Council had held that an attempt to abolish appeals to itself in criminal matters, by the federal Parliament, was unconstitutional. In the British Coal Corporation decision, however, which took place after the passage of the Statute of Westminster, the Court changed its position and held that the abolition of criminal appeals to the Privy Council was constitutional. In the course of that decision Viscount Sankey stated that the Dominion legislature was supreme and endowed "with the same authority as the Imperial Parliament, within the assigned limits of subject and area, just as it was said in Hodge v. The Queen that Section 92 of the Act had that effect in regard to the provincial legislatures."[28]

The Court was able to change the decision in the Naden case because of the provision in the Statute of Westminster that the Colonial Laws Validity Act, 1865, was no longer to apply to any statute passed by the federal Parliament. The Colonial Laws Validity Act had acted as a restriction on the exercise of parliamentary supremacy of the federal Parliament, in that it had provided that any federal enactment that was contrary to a British statute specifically applying to the Dominion rendered the Dominion statute unconstitutional. This was a clear restriction on the supremacy of the federal Parliament which, as the Judicial Committee pointed out in the British Coal Corporation case, was now removed by the Statute of Westminster. In addition, the Statute of Westminster had removed another ground for the decision in the Naden case, namely, the argument that Canada's Parliament could not pass extra-territorial legislation.

With these two basic restrictions on federal legislative authority removed, the Judicial Committee was inspired, in the British Coal Corporation case, not only to state that the federal Parliament was within its sphere supreme, but also to suggest that the federal Parliament and the provincial legislatures had, between them, a totality of legislative power for Canada. Lord Sankey did, however, refer to the fact that this totality of self-government was still limited by the terms of the Statute of Westminster, which prohibited amendments to the British North America Act, 1867-1930, by the federal Parliament. In several instances, such as Bank of Toronto v. Lambe, the Privy Council has stated that "The Federation Act exhausts the whole range of legislative power."[29] This statement was not technically true when originally made, and is still not true today, as a number of important matters dealt with in the British North America Act, 1867 can only be changed by a legislative enactment of the British Parliament. For all practical purposes, however, this Parliament will only act upon a request of the Canadian government which, in turn, has usually requested the approval of the provinces before seeking important amendments to the British North America Act. This is a technical restriction on the doctrine of exhaustiveness — that is to say, that the federal Parliament and provincial legislatures control between them the whole area of self-government. This is a technical restriction because, in fact, the United Kingdom Parliament will amend the British North America Act if requested to do so by Canada. Are there any other restrictions on this doctrine, that the federal Parliament and the provincial legislatures between them have a totality of legislative power?

One restriction on the combined legal power of the two legislatures is their inability to delegate to each other. Owing to the decision in the Nova Scotia case,[30] the federal Parliament cannot delegate its authority to a provincial legislature, and a provincial legislature cannot delegate its authority to the federal Parliament. This was a surprising decision, since it was one of the few occasions when a Canadian court rejected the full implications of the doctrine of the supremacy of Parliament. The real basis of the Supreme Court of Canada decision was that a delegation of this kind was incompatible with the existence of a federal system. In addition, arguments were put forward to the effect that a provincial legislature or Parliament did not have the power to accept this type of delegation. It was stressed that the people of Canada have a right to expect that the members they elect to the federal House will deliberate on federal matters, and members elected to the provincial Assembly will deliberate on provincial matters.

Nova Scotia's Supreme Court, in its decision on the matter,[31] dealt with this question somewhat more fully than did the Supreme Court of Canada. For example, Chief Justice Chisholm argued that, since there was no express power permitting such an inter-delegation, therefore it must be prohibited. Secondly, he argued that the use of the word "exclusively," at the beginning of Section 92, meant that powers vested in the provincial legislature were to be exercised by that body alone. Furthermore, Chief Justice Chisholm voiced the argument, which was also implicit in some of the judgments of members of the Supreme Court, that delegation involves subordination and, therefore, since neither of the legislative levels in Canada, either federal or provincial, is subordinate, one to the other, delegation between them is impossible. Another very interesting line of argument was advanced by Chief Justice Chisholm when he compared our constitutional system with that of the United States. He argued that the American pattern was in the minds of the Fathers of Confederation when they formulated our constitution. From this assumption he concluded that, since inter-delegation is not permitted in the American constitutional system, therefore we must assume that it is not permissible within the Canadian framework. This is, in our view, a very misleading argument, because it suggests that there is in existence a perfect federal model, and that any deviation from this model should be regarded as illegal. This approach is especially disconcerting when it is realized that the Fathers of Confederation looked at the American Constitution, but they did so with the object of trying to ascertain the weaknesses in the American system, so that these could be avoided in Canada's new constitutional system. Each constitution must be read subject to its *own* national context. There is considerable danger in supposing that the assumptions of one constitutional system are the same as those of another. This is not to say that one should never benefit from the experience or the judicial reasoning of other jurisdictions, but to slavishly try to fit one's own constitution into a mold established by another country is equally dangerous.

Surprisingly, only Mr. Justice Doull of the Nova Scotia Supreme Court dissented from the view that the federal Parliament and the provincial legislature of Nova Scotia cannot delegate powers to each other. He assumed that the provincial legislature is supreme within its sphere and, therefore, can delegate its powers to anyone it chooses. Furthermore, he made it very clear that delegation does not constitute a giving away of power, but is merely a temporary permission for certain designated delegatees to exercise power until such time as the legislature withdraws it from them. To him, this did not involve any question of subordination, but was consistent with the traditional view that, since the legislature is supreme within its sphere, it can temporarily vest whichever of its powers it wishes to any delegatee that it chooses. He underlined the fact that ultimate power still resides exclusively with the delegating body, and the delegation can be revoked any time the delegating body wishes. Thus, he did not feel there was any violation of the scheme of the British North America Act, in that there was no change in the basic powers allotted to either the federal Parliament or, in this case, the legislature of Nova Scotia. It is our view that not only are Mr. Justice Doull's conclusions socially and politically more desirable than the majority conclusions but also his position logically follows the decisions and reasons for judgment handed down in *Hodge v. The Queen* and *British Coal Corporation v. The King*. Nevertheless, the decision was clear and interdelegation is prohibited in Canada. It must, therefore, be added to those powers which even the federal Parliament and the provincial legislatures, acting together, do not have.

Another probable limitation on the doctrine of exhaustiveness is the inability of Canadian legislatures to change the office of Lieutenant-Governor. Section 92 (1) specifically provides that the provincial legislatures have control over their own constitutions "except as regards the office of Lieutenant-Governor." Since this constitutional area is forbidden to the provinces, are we to assume that it comes within federal legislative jurisdiction? It is our view that, since the present amending section of the Act (91 (1)) provides that matters coming within the British North America Act relating to "rights or privileges by this or any other Constitutional Act granted or secured to the Legislature or the Government of a province" are not amendable by the federal Parliament, then the office of Lieutenant-Governor is a right or privilege granted by the British North America Act to the provinces, and could not be changed except by a statute amending the British North America Act passed by the United Kingdom Parliament. It is thus our view that the office of Lieutenant-Governor is another area of self-government which, in a technical legal sense, is denied to both the federal Parliament and the provincial legislature, separately or by joint legal action.

It should also be noted that the provincial legislatures, though granted authority over education, cannot pass any law which prejudicially affects "any Right or Privilege with respect to Denominational Schools which any Class of Persons have by Law in the Province at the

Union."[32] This means that the provincial legislature is denied the right to legislate in such a way as to deprive certain persons of their denominational school rights. Though Section 93 (4) allows the federal Parliament to pass remedial laws necessary to restore educational rights denied by a provincial statute or decision, nevertheless, this subsection does not allow Parliament to change the guaranteed denominational school rights protected in Section 93 (1). Thus, we have another area of subject matter which is denied to the provincial legislatures and to the federal Parliament, acting either singly or together.

One could probably find other restrictions on the exhaustiveness of federal-provincial legislative power, but the foregoing are sufficient to show the danger of a glib statement that they possess a totality of legislative power. It must be kept in mind, however, that we are dealing here, essentially, with legal restrictions on the totality of legislative power. In reality, there is no area of the British North America Act that could not be changed, if the federal Parliament and the provincial legislatures decided to bring about change by requesting the British Parliament to amend the British North America Act. For example, acting upon the request of the Canadian government, the United Kingdom Parliament could amend the British North America Act to permit inter-delegation or to change the office of Lieutenant-Governor, or even to deny protection to denominational schools under Section 93. Thus, one can say that, in practice, it would be relatively simple for Canada to exercise a totality of power in any area it wished; nevertheless, as the constitution stands at present, there are matters that cannot be changed either by the federal Parliament or the provincial legislatures, acting alone or in conjunction with each other. The translation of reality into practice will only come after the adoption of an amending process which does not require resort to the United Kingdom Parliament. As will be explained later, repeated attempts to develop a purely domestic amending formula have been unsuccessful. It is interesting to note that the Fulton-Favreau proposals in connection with a purely domestic amending formula included a provision which would permit inter-delegation between the different legislative levels.

It is now necessary to re-examine the doctrine of the supremacy of Parliament as it has purportedly applied to legislation enacted by the federal Parliament or the provincial legislatures. As already indicated, this is the principle which, as defined by Dicey, means that a parliament has the right to pass or repeal any law, and that no other authoritative body can overrule or render null a parliamentary enactment. Two decisions have already been examined which state that, within their jurisdiction as defined by the British North America Act, the legislatures of the provinces and the federal Parliament are supreme. This, in essence, would mean that, once the courts have decided that legislation has been passed by the appropriate legislature under the terms dividing power in the British North America Act, then they have no authority whatsoever to challenge the validity of the statute. The impact of this doctrine essentially means that the judiciary cannot, as in the United States, strike down legislation as being unconstitutional, unless one of the legislative bodies is acting outside the area of power assigned to it by the British North America Act.

Earlier in this work it was pointed out that the courts have evolved a set of rules of statutory interpretation which they apply to any act before them. As already outlined, these rules can be very effectively used to blunt the full impact of a statute, particularly by the use of a series of presumptions which the courts assume, in the absence of very express language to the contrary, the legislature did not intend to abrogate. Canadian courts, however, have, on the whole, been very much influenced by the doctrine of the supremacy of Parliament, subject always, of course, to the basic principle that the statute must be passed by a legislature acting within its assigned jurisdiction under the British North America Act. This has been one of the reasons why there was, for a considerable period of time in Canada, a demand that there be entrenched in the Constitution a bill of rights — that is to say, that there should be an area of power denied to both the federal and provincial legislatures: in effect, an implementation, in the constitution, of the traditional theories of natural law developed largely by the English political theorist, John Locke. He essentially argued that government was a contract between the rulers and the ruled, and that part of the terms of this contract involves denial of certain powers to the ruling establishment. This concept of Locke's was implemented in the United States by the inclusion of the Bill of Rights in the constitution. The American courts, through their role as interpreters of the constitution, especially the applicability of the Bill of Rights, have, in effect, become the custodians of what are the ultimate values of the American nation. In the absence of an entrenched bill of rights in the Canadian Constitutional system, the Canadian courts have not been willing to exercise a role comparable to that of the American judiciary. It is, however, still possible that the Canadian Bill of Rights will be utilized by the legal profession and the judiciary in the creation of more activist courts. This question will be discussed more fully at the end of this chapter.

Parliamentary supremacy is a doctrine which has not proved as frightening in its implementation as it appears in theory. First, it must be recognized that the greatest restraint on legislative action is public opinion. This has meant that the Canadian legislatures have, on the whole, never abused the very widespread power vested in them. Furthermore, experience has shown that theoretical rights in a nation's constitution mean very little if the people of that country are indifferent to the protection of these rights.

Let us now examine the doctrine of political supremacy, and a few instances in which the doctrine has either been challenged or its limits defined. In the case of In Re George Gray,[33] Mr. Gray sought a writ of habeas corpus, seeking to obtain his release from the Armed Services of Canada. Gray had been granted exemption from military service under the conditions of the Military Service Act. Subsequent to his exemption under this Act, an order-in-council was passed abolishing the class of exemption into which Mr. Gray fitted. This order-in-council, passed by the Cabinet, was an exercise of the power delegated to the Governor-in-Council (in effect, the Cabinet) by Parliament under the terms of the War Measures Act. The whole question of war and civil liberties in Canada will be dealt with later in this work; it is sufficient here to say that, at the time of the Gray case, the War Measures Act delegated to the Governor-in-Council virtually total power for the conduct of the Canadian war effort. It meant that the Cabinet, by virtue of this delegation, could pass regulations having the effect of law on any subject which related to the conduct of the war. Counsel for Gray argued that the power to make rules and regulations by virtue of delegation to the Governor-in-Council should not be extended to allow that body to legislate. The essence of the argument was that Parliament had essentially amended the constitution by delegating, almost totally, its legislative responsibilities. The essential question is, under the doctrine of supremacy of Parliament, how far can Parliament go in delegating its authority? Surely, if it is genuinely supreme within its sphere, then it can delegate any power it wishes. Gray's Counsel essentially argued that there were limits on this power, and that the constitution provided that major legislative power should reside with Parliament and not with a delegatee.

The Supreme Court of Canada rejected the arguments of Gray's Counsel, and held that the order-in-council passed by the Cabinet under the War Measures Act rendered Gray liable for military service, despite his previous exemption under the Military Service Act. It should be mentioned, however, that the Military Service Act included a provision to the effect that "nothing in this Act shall be held to limit or affect . . . the powers of the Governor in Council under the War Measures Act." Chief Justice Fitzpatrick denied that there was any separation of powers as part of the law of the Canadian constitution but, instead, pointed out that though Parliament cannot abdicate its functions, nevertheless, "within reasonable limits at any rate it can delegate its powers to the executive government. Such powers must necessarily be subject to determination at any time by parliament. . . ."[34] He stated that he could see no restriction within the British North America Act which "would impose any limitation on the authority of the Parliament of Canada to which the Imperial Parliament is not subject."[35] Presumably he recognized the division of legislative powers, and was assessing federal parliamentary power subject to exercise within the appropriate jurisdiction. Mr. Justice Duff reiterated the comments of the Chief Justice that Parliament could not "abandon any of its own legislative jurisdiction."[36] He also pointed out that the powers granted to the Governor-General-in-Council were defined by and were under the control of Parliament and could be withdrawn at any time Parliament wished. He argued that the War Measures Act did not constitute an abandonment of any legislative authority, or of any intention to abandon control in the future. Mr. Justice Anglin stated that a complete abdication by Parliament of its legislative responsibility was incon-

37

ceivable, and then went on to say, "Short of such an abdication any limited delegation would seem to be within the ambit of a legislative jurisdiction. . . ."[37] It is interesting to compare Mr. Justice Anglin's proposition that anything short of an abdication is permissible with his phrase that "any limited delegation" is acceptable.

A similar sort of qualification appears in the judgment of the Chief Justice where, after seemingly stating that the only limit on delegation is that the legislature cannot abandon its functions, he then made the very peculiar statement that "within reasonable limits at any rate it can delegate its powers to the executive government."[38] One cannot but speculate on what is the difference between reasonable limits and the point at which the delegation constitutes an abdication of functions. It would seem that the area of restraint posed by such words as "reasonable limits" and "limited delegation" would constitute a much more severe restriction than permitting Parliament to delegate under any circumstances short of abdication. Furthermore, there is no attempt to define what is meant by the term "abdication," though the implication is that as long as Parliament has the power to both withdraw the delegation and to alter its terms, then there is no abdication. One could only assume that the qualifying remarks in the judgment of the Chief Justice and of Mr. Justice Anglin were a result of a fear of the full implication of what they had said about Parliament's right to delegation. They were perhaps somewhat frightened by their own proposition that delegation was permissible in any circumstances short of abdication. They were perhaps anxious to lay some tentative groundwork to enable future courts to hold that there was some degree of limitation on this very widespread power. The essential fact, however, is that the court upheld the tremendously wide delegation which took place under the War Measures Act and, therefore, this type of delegation was considered to be "within reasonable limits." Accordingly, there seems to be very little restriction on the federal legislative authority to delegate.

Furthermore, the question of whether it is possible for Parliament to abdicate its functions should be raised. One of the essential elements of the concept of the supremacy of Parliament is that Parliament cannot be bound by its previous legislation. If carried to its logical conclusion this would mean that if one Parliament attempted to abdicate its authority, another Parliament could revoke this attempt. Considerable theorizing could centre around this rather abstract question, however, for if the situation ever developed where a virtual abdication did take place, it would be such an extraordinary political situation that the normal ground rules of the constitutional system in Canada would possibly no longer be operative. In this event, technical arguments about whether Parliament can bind itself or not would probably be irrelevant.

The essential result of the Gray decision is that there are, in fact, very few, if any, limits on Parliament's power to delegate its legislative authority, subject, of course, to the qualification that the courts might resist any attempt to give authority to a body over which Parliament was no longer to have control. Since this is a virtually inconceivable situation, it means, in effect, that the Gray decision allows Parliament almost unlimited authority to delegate its legislative powers without the fear of challenge by the courts. Certainly no other decisions rendered either in the First or Second World War constitute a serious challenge to the decision in the Gray case. Perhaps the one notable exception is a decision by a county court judge in the case of *R. v. Holmes*,[39] where it was held that the re-delegation by the Cabinet of the authority delegated to it by Parliament under the War Measures Act was invalid.

The Government was so disturbed by this decision it immediately submitted a reference to the Supreme Court of Canada, known as *Reference re Regulation re Chemicals*.[40] The regulation in question was a test regulation passed by the Controller of Chemicals, under authority re-delegated to him by the Governor-General-in-Council, whose authority in turn had been delegated by Parliament under the War Measures Act. The Supreme Court of Canada unanimously upheld the validity of the regulation. This, in effect, meant that not only is Parliament entitled to delegate most of its legislative authority to the Cabinet, but that it is also permissible for the Cabinet to re-delegate its authority to another delegatee.

The argument was made in the Chemicals case that a delegate cannot re-delegate, or, as this proposition is usually phrased, *delegatus non potest delegare*. The Court, in our view, quite rightly maintained that this is purely a maxim of statutory interpretation and only a presumption against delegation which the Court will read into any statute. In the event, however, that it is obvious, either by clear language or by express implication, that re-delegation is necessary for carrying out the objective of the statute, the Court will permit it. In this particular case, the Court felt that re-delegation was within the scope and object of the statute and was necessary for its implementation and accordingly found that this re-delegation of authority to the Controller of Chemicals was valid. It might be argued that these are rather exceptional cases and that they were rendered in time of war; nevertheless, they have given us an opportunity to examine what the courts would regard as the limits of the power of the federal Parliament to delegate. It seems fairly clear that, if the parliamentary language is specific, this power of delegation is virtually unlimited. This widespread parliamentary authority, however, is perfectly consistent with the doctrine of the supremacy of Parliament.

It is, however, interesting to contrast this decision with another one rendered in peace time by the Supreme Court of Canada. In *Attorney-General of Canada v. Brent*,[41] the Supreme Court of Canada held invalid a deportation order made by a special enquiry officer appointed under the existing Canadian Immigration Act. In this particular case the Parliament of Canada had delegated widespread authority to the Cabinet to define the classes of persons eligible for immigration to Canada. This authority was, except for one or two words, re-delegated verbatim to a number of special enquiry officers in various parts of Canada. The Supreme Court of Canada upheld the Ontario

Court of Appeal's decision of invalidity on the ground that a virtually verbatim re-delegation of Cabinet powers was not contemplated by Parliament at the time it delegated this power of making immigration regulations to the Governor General-in-Council. The Court was obviously perturbed that this re-delegation would be given to a wide variety of different people, all of whom would interpret their authority in a different way. There was no suggestion, however, on the part of either the Court of Appeal of Ontario or the Supreme Court of Canada that if this power had been simply re-delegated to one Controller of Immigration, they would have held that invalid. Furthermore, if Parliament had specifically indicated that the exact authority vested in the Governor General-in-Council could be re-delegated to a number of immigration officers, it is probably unlikely that the Court would have resisted this clear statement of parliamentary purpose.

The decision is interesting, however, in illustrating, not the theoretical limits of parliamentary authority, but rather the fact that a determined court can, even in a system dedicated to the concept of parliamentary supremacy, use rules of statutory interpretation to prevent what it considers to be undesirable results. It is always relatively simple for a court to hold that the intention of Parliament is not completely clear, or that what has taken place is not within the scope and object of the legislation. It is also obvious that the courts are more willing to approach a statute in this way in time of peace than they are in time of war, when the trend of judicial decision-making in both Canada and Great Britain was quite clearly to uphold the validity of legislation and the methods of its implementation.

It has been suggested by one writer, G. S. Rutherford, that there is a greater restriction on the right of the provinces to delegate their authority than there is with respect to the federal Parliament.[42] This would, accordingly, suggest that there is a restriction on the supremacy of the provincial legislatures, acting within their sphere, which does not apply to the federal Parliament. Mr. Rutherford's argument is that since, by virtue of Section 92 (1), the province is forbidden to change the office of Lieutenant-Governor, any delegation of legislative functions would affect his office, in the sense that he would no longer be required to sign the resultant legislative rules passed by the provincial cabinet. There is limited judicial support for this line of argument, the leading case being a decision of the Court of Appeal of Alberta, *Credit Foncier v. Ross*.[43] In this case the Alberta legislature had passed a statute known as the Reduction and Settlement of Debts Acts. This statute was part of a series of legislation, passed by the newly elected Social Credit government in the mid 1930's, designed, in their view, to protect the ordinary Albertan from the financial establishment. This particular act provided for the reduction and settlement of certain debts. It listed a number of debts which could be reduced, and followed this with a phrase which read that the Lieutenant-Governor-in-Council could declare any debt to be "a debt to which this Act does not apply."

The Act was declared *ultra vires* at trial, and an appeal was taken by the Attorney-General of the province. The Court of Appeal of Alberta held that the statute was *ultra vires* the provincial legislature on the grounds, first, that it added to the functions of the Lieutenant-Governor and therefore was legislation respecting his office, and second — of particular interest in this context — that it vested in the Lieutenant-Governor-in-Council the authority to pass legislation itself. Quoting from *Hodge v. The Queen*, the Court pointed out how, in that case, the Privy Council had stated that the power to delegate authority is "ancillary to legislation," and went on to say that there is an abundance of examples of delegation "entrusting a limited discretionary authority to others." The Court seized upon the word, "ancillary," from the Hodge case, and said that the delegation in the statute before them was not the right to pass regulations ancillary to legislation but was, in fact, a taking over of the legislative function itself and, by virtue of the remarks in the Hodge case, illegal. Furthermore, the Court argued that the power of disallowance was given to the Governor General-in-Council, with respect to acts of the provincial legislatures, and that legislation of this kind, which allowed wide-scale rule-making by the Lieutenant-Governor-in-Council, in effect circumvented the power of disallowance vested in the Governor General-in-Council. It referred to the decision of the Supreme Court of Canada in the Gray case, and admitted that there was in that case a delegation of legislative authority to the Governor General-in-Council. The Court, however, distinguished this case on the ground that it was passed during war time and, therefore, was not applicable in this situation. The Court said, quite specifically, "This is neither a war measure nor is it Dominion legislation, so the case cited would appear to have no application." The phrase "nor is it Dominion legislation" seems to suggest that there may be vested in the federal Parliament wider areas of power to delegate than with the provincial legislatures. This statement would be of considerable significance if it had reflected judicial opinion for a number of years before, or if it had been followed by subsequent courts. The general trend, however, has been that the courts have upheld provincial legislative delegation as readily as they have done for the federal Parliament.

In one other case, *Hayward v. British Columbia Lower Mainland Dairy Products Board*,[44] a trial judge, Mr. Justice Manson, expressed a point of view similar to the Court of Appeal in Alberta, basing his language, just as that Court had done, on the language in the Hodge case, suggesting that delegation is valid only with respect to matters ancillary to legislation. There again, Mr. Justice Manson distinguished the Gray case on the grounds that perhaps the federal Parliament has wider powers of delegation than the provincial legislatures have. Furthermore, in the Hayward case, Mr. Justice Manson denied the right of the legislature to delegate wide-scale powers under the Natural Products Marketing (B.C.) Act, on the ground that it constituted a delegation of legislative function which, he suggested, was contrary to the general scheme of the British North America Act. He argued that this Act was designed to provide for separation of powers between the legislative, executive, and judicial branches of government, and that this delegation of legislative power departed from this basic scheme. This is a very extreme statement, as there is very little to suggest that there is, in fact, any desire to have in Canada the rigid separation of powers that exists in the United States. In fact, the doctrine of parliamentary supremacy is really the key factor in preventing the development of such a system, in that, under the supremacy doctrine, in the United Kingdom the courts and the executive are all, in legal theory, totally subordinate to the will of the United Kingdom Parliament, or, in Canada, to either the federal or provincial legislatures, if acting within their proper spheres.

In an appeal to the British Columbia Court of Appeal,[45] the Court refused to uphold the decision of Mr. Justice Manson. The judgment was, however, a very unsatisfactory one, as it did not adequately deal with the rather extreme statements made by the trial judge. In fact, there were one or two phrases in the Court of Appeal judgment which seemed, by implication, to theoretically support Mr. Justice Manson, and which suggested that no constitutional principles were violated in this case. For example, Mr. Justice MacDonald stated, "There is no abrogation of legislative authority." He went on to say, "The main Act is not merely a skeleton Act without any substantive statement of policy or intent."[46] The implication one gets is that there could be delegation, which would imply an abrogation of legislative authority. What does the word "abrogation" mean? Is this the same thing as "abdication"? Are there limits on provincial legislative authority that do not exist with respect to the federal Parliament? Certainly if the word "abrogation" is a greater limitation than "abdication" we must draw this conclusion.

The case was appealed to the Judicial Committee of the Privy Council.[47] The decision of the Privy Council was very disappointing on the point just previously discussed, and merely stated that, "Within the appointed sphere the provincial legislature is as supreme as any other parliament; and it is unnecessary to try to enumerate the innumerable occasions on which legislatures, provincial, Dominion and Imperial, have entrusted various persons and bodies with similar powers to those contained in this Act."[48] The essence of this statement is that if it has been done before it must be legal, which is a rather unsatisfactory method of dealing with a constitutional problem. The end result of this case, however, was to justify the delegation of very widespread powers for the control of marketing in British Columbia to the Lieutenant-Governor-in-Council. As already pointed out, the Credit Foncier case and the decision of Mr. Justice Manson in the Hayward case are really exceptions, as the trend has certainly been to uphold all provincial delegation on very much the same grounds and, to the same extent, as federal delegation. Most of the judiciary undoubtedly assume that, within its sphere, the provincial legislature is, as has already been pointed out, supreme and therefore, by implication, can delegate whatever of its power it wishes.

During war time, the trend seemed to be that the courts were unwilling to strike down the validity of federal legislation, but before this they were willing to render unconstitutional the series of enactments first passed by the Social Credit Government of Alberta when it came to power in 1935. The Social Credit legislation of that time, which struck very hard at the financial community, was roughly treated by the courts. The decision in the Credit Foncier case is a reflection of the willingness of Canadian courts to be active and use various judicial tools when they regard legislation as particularly undesirable. Most of the Social Credit legislation was struck down by the courts on the grounds that these statutes invaded the federal legislative field, but in the Credit Foncier case it is interesting to note that other methods for rendering the legislation invalid were used. The courts have been willing to use the techniques of statutory interpretation, declaring legislation ultra vires or outside provincial or federal jurisdiction, and in only very rare instances to suggest limits on the power of Parliament to delegate, as methods of judicial control of legislative action.

There is, however, an interesting and very rare pronouncement by a Supreme Court judge that there might be a right vested in the Canadian courts to declare that certain types of activity could not be prohibited by either the federal or the provincial legislatures. This statement, by Mr. Justice Abbott, was made in his reasons for judgment in the case of *Switzman v. Elbling*.[49] In that case the plaintiff sued for the cancellation of a lease made with the defendant, arguing that there had been a breach of a Quebec provincial statute on the part of the defendant. The statute (commonly referred to as the Padlock Act) was entitled "An Act to Protect the Province against Communistic Propaganda,"[50] the alleged purpose of which was to control communist activities within the province. The Act provided that it was illegal for any person who possessed or occupied a house in the province of Quebec to use it for the purpose of propagating communism. It allowed the Attorney-General, on being satisfied that a house was being used for the above purpose, to order the closing of this house, though it gave the owner the right to petition a judge of the Superior Court to have the order reviewed. As a result of this statute the premises, which were being leased from the plaintiff, were closed pursuant to the terms of this Act. The defendant, upon being sued for cancellation of his lease, argued that the provincial statute was unconstitutional. This argument was rejected by the trial judge and was also rejected by the highest appeal court in the province of Quebec, namely the Court of Queen's Bench.[51]

An appeal was then taken to the Supreme Court of Canada on the ground that this legislation was ultra vires the provincial legislature. It is sufficient for our purposes to state that the Act was declared unconstitutional on the grounds that it was legislation in respect of criminal law which, under the terms of the British North America Act, is a subject assigned to the federal Parliament. Mr. Justice Abbott agreed with his colleagues that this was legislation in respect of criminal law, but went on to state that:

> Although it is not necessary, of course, to determine this question
> for the purposes of the present appeal, the Canadian Constitution
> being declared to be similar in principle to that of the United King-

dom, I am also of opinion that as our constitutional law stands Parliament itself could not abrogate this right of discussion and debate. The power of Parliament to limit it is, in my view, restricted to such powers as may be exercisable under its exclusive legislative jurisdiction with respect to criminal law and to make laws for the peace, order and good government of the nation.[52]

This was a most unusual pronouncement for a Canadian judge, as it runs contrary to the general thesis that within a legislature's sphere, as defined by the British North America Act, it is supreme. It should be noted that to justify his statement, Mr. Justice Abbott referred to a portion of the preamble of the British North America Act, namely that Canada is to have a "Constitution similar in Principle to that of the United Kingdom." On the other hand, there is no concept more fundamental to the British Constitution than that of supremacy of Parliament, which would lead one to a conclusion directly opposite from that outlined by Mr. Justice Abbott. As the learned judge himself admitted, his proposition was not the fundamental reason for his decision and was, therefore, obiter dicta and, accordingly, not binding on lower courts in the Canadian judicial hierarchy. It might, however, be effectively used as a basis for argument by lower courts in the event that they were desperate to render an enactment ineffective in some particular situation. It has not yet, to the best of our knowledge, been used by any Canadian judges, and is unlikely to form the basis of judicial reasoning in Canada except in some extraordinary situation.

There is at least one other judicial pronouncement which comes very close to the type of position taken by Mr. Justice Abbott in the Padlock case. This is a statement made by Mr. Justice Casey in the Chabot case.[53] In this case the appellant was a member of the Jehovah's Witnesses, a religious order. His two children had been attending public school in Lamorendière, Quebec. Since the district was almost exclusively Roman Catholic, the school was run according to the course of study laid down by the Roman Catholic Committee of the Quebec Council of Public Instruction. It was required by this course of study that students should pass examinations not only in secular subjects but in religious subjects as well. Mr. Chabot asked that his children be relieved from attending the religious courses because they were not members of the Roman Catholic faith. Ultimately they were expelled from the school on the ground that they would not attend these prescribed religious courses. Mr. Chabot took legal action, seeking a judicial declaration that the provisions of the statute (in this case the Education Act and the regulations made thereunder), as they affected his children, were illegal. The highest appeal court in the province of Quebec, the Court of Queen's Bench, overruled the trial judge and held that the children were not required to attend the courses in Roman Catholic religious instruction. Four of the seven judges, namely Hyde, Martineau, Taschereau and Owen, J.J., held that, under the very special educational situation in Quebec at that time, though in fact it was run as a Catholic School under the jurisdiction of the Catholic Committee, nevertheless, de jure, the school was non-denominational. Very briefly, in the Quebec system at that time it was customary to place a school under the jurisdiction of a provincial Catholic or Protestant Education Committee. In a district where the number of the minority did not justify a separate school, it meant that all children would have to attend that single school, even if they were not of the faith of the majority. Thus, the Court stated in this particular case that, because nearly all the students were Catholic, the Catholic Committee had jurisdiction for the purposes of prescribing curriculum, yet, because there was no Protestant school in the area, in law the school was considered a common school. On this ground, therefore, the Chabot children could not be forced to attend religious instruction at what was, in a strict legal sense, a non-denominational school. Thus, the majority were able to say that the Education Act of the province did not allow school boards of common schools to impose religious instruction on all children irrespective of their faith.

The interesting part of this case, however, is not the narrow technical point on which the decision was reached, but rather a position taken by Mr. Justice Casey in his judgment. He argued that it is a basic human right that a child cannot be compelled to attend religious instruction or religious exercises if it is not the faith of his parents. He took the view that there are certain rights which "find their existence in the very nature of man," and that these rights "must prevail should they conflict with the provisions of positive law."[54] This statement was not necessary to the judicial conclusion reached by Mr. Justice Casey, but he was prepared, if necessary, to hold a statute unconstitutional on the grounds that it violated the principles of a higher natural law. This statement is similar in its effect to that made by Mr. Justice Abbott in the Switzman and Elbling case referred to earlier, though it must be emphasized that both of these comments were made in passing by the two judges concerned, and were not basic or essential to the decision which they reached.

Mr. Justice Hyde, with whom Martineau, J. concurred, also made a very interesting comment in the Chabot case, though it is not quite as clear as Mr. Justice Casey's. Mr. Justice Hyde stated as follows, "The power given to the Roman Catholic Committee to determine the course of studies in the schools under its jurisdiction cannot be construed to override this basic principle of natural law. It would require very specific provisions in the Act to that effect to justify any such interpretation and then, of course, the constitutionality of such provisions would be a matter for consideration."[55] This statement admittedly is not as bold as that of Mr. Justice Casey, and tends to suggest that very clear provisions in the Act would serve to override the proposition that children should not be compelled to take religious instruction in a faith which is not theirs or that of their family. It is interesting to note, however, his use of the term "natural law" and the phrase that even though there were specific provisions in the Act the "constitutionality of such provisions would be a matter for consideration." It is rather difficult to ascertain exactly what this latter phrase means, though it seems unlikely that Mr. Justice Hyde would have been willing to go as far as Mr. Justice Casey in the face of very clear language in the statute. The position taken by Mr. Justice Casey is, in fact, a position considerably more extreme than that adopted by the American judiciary, who render their judgments on the constitutionality of statutes on the basis of whether they violate the prohibited terms of the positive law of the constitution. Mr. Justice Casey was willing to declare positive law unconstitutional on the ground that it violated certain inherent rights found in some higher law. Presumably these rights would be defined by the judge concerned. It seems to us rather dangerous to allow each judge, on his own initiative, without resort to a bill of rights or similar positive enactment, to declare unconstitutional any positive law which he feels violates some supposedly more basic code of ethics. This, however, raises a complex question of legal philosophy which cannot be fully explored at the present time. It is hoped, however, to comment somewhat more on this issue when dealing, in later sections of this book, with the question of the role of the judiciary in relation to civil liberties.

It is imperative at this point to comment on two Supreme Court of Canada decisions dealing with the question of the extent to which the Bill of Rights should be used to override other federal statutes or portions thereof. To date (1975), the major case utilizing the Bill of Rights is that of *Regina v. Drybones*.[56] In that case Joseph Drybones, an Indian, was charged with violating section 94 (b) of the Indian Act in that he was "an Indian who is intoxicated off a reserve." Ironically, there is no reservation within the meaning of the Indian Act in the Northwest Territories. The incident took place in Yellowknife where Drybones was found intoxicated on the steps of a hotel. Originally convicted and fined ten dollars, his conviction was overturned by the Territorial Court and this decision was sustained by the Court of Appeal of the Northwest Territories. This decision was appealed by The Crown to the Supreme Court of Canada. By a majority of six to three the Court rejected the appeal of the Crown and in effect used Section 1 (b) of the Canadian Bill of Rights to override and render inoperative Section 94 (b) of the Indian Act. Section 1 (b) of the Bill of Rights outlines "the right of the individual to equality before the law and the protection of the law." Thus the Court was taking the unusual step of declaring invalid a piece of federal legislation without resorting to an argument based on the division of legislative powers.

A number of commentators saw this decision as a turning point in the evolution of Canadian law. They envisaged this case as being a first step in the development of a more activist judiciary using the Bill of Rights to strike down federal legislation contrary to its terms. It was envisaged that the Supreme Court would begin to play a role in Canada similar to that played by the Supreme Court in the United States. The most recent decision of the Supreme Court, however, has not confirmed this impression.

In the *Attorney-General of Canada v. Lavell*,[57] Mrs. Lavell, an Indian, married a non-Indian, which resulted in her name being struck from the Indian Register. This action was taken pursuant to the specific provisions of Section 12 (1) (b) of the Indian Act. This section provides that any Indian woman married to a non-Indian is not entitled to be registered as an Indian under the Act. Mrs. Lavell asked the Court to declare Section 12 (1) (b) of the Indian Act inoperative as discriminating between Indian men and women and thus as being in conflict with Section 1 (b) of the Bill of Rights. The basis of her argument was that the Indian Act does not require the expunging of the name of a male Indian who marries a non-Indian woman. This argument was rejected by the Supreme Court. By a five to four majority, the Court held that to allow the Bill of Rights to prevail over the specific terms of the Indian Act would amount to allowing an abrogation of Parliament's power over Indians as conferred by Section 91 (24) of the B.N.A. Act. This is in effect a re-statement of an oft-stated judicial principle concerning the Bill of Rights, namely that the specific wording of a federal statute will take precedence over the more general wording of the Bill of Rights.

The decision in the Lavell case supports both in theory and in practice the doctrine of supremacy of Parliament. Even if the Court had reached a result similar to that of the majority in the Drybones case, it would not have overturned this doctrine because the Bill of Rights itself is only an ordinary Act of Parliament amendable or subject to repeal by Parliament. A continuation, however, of the position taken in Drybones would have had the practical, if not the theoretical effect of moving the country away from ultimate legislative authority. Mr. Justice Abbott, in his dissenting opinion in the Lavell case, neatly summarizes this position when he states:

> In my view the Canadian Bill of Rights has substantially affected the doctrine of the supremacy of Parliament. Like any other statute it can of course be repealed or amended, or a particular law declared to be applicable notwithstanding the provisions of the Bill. In form the supremacy of Parliament is maintained but in practice I think that it has been substantially curtailed. In my opinion that result is undesirable, but that is a matter for consideration by Parliament not the Courts.
>
> Ritchie, J., said in his reasons for judgment in Drybones, that the implementation of the Bill of Rights by the Courts can give rise to great difficulties and that statement has been borne out in subsequent litigation. Of one thing I am certain the Bill will continue to supply ample grist to the judicial mills for some time to come.

REFERENCES

1. *British North America Act, 1867*, 30-31 Vict., C.3 (U.K.) (hereinafter referred to as B.N.A. Act).
2. *B.N.A. Act, 1949*, 13 Geo. VI, C.81 (U.K.).
3. *B.N.A. Act, 1940*, 3-4 Geo. VI, C.36 (U.K.).
4. *B.N.A. Act, 1951*, 14-15 Geo. VI, C.32 (U.K.).
5. *B.N.A. Act, 1960*, 9 Elizabeth II, C.2 (U.K.).
6. *B.N.A. Act, 1965*, S.C., 1965, C.4.
7. *Statute of Westminster, 1931*, 22 Geo. V, C.4 (U.K.).
8. *B.N.A. Act, 1867*, S. 37.
9. *B.N.A. Act, 1867*, S. 21.

10. See R. A. Mackay, *The Unreformed Senate of Canada*, rev. ed. McClelland and Stewart, Toronto, 1963, ch. 11, pp. 173-89; F. A. Kunz, *The Modern Senate of Canada 1925-1963: A Reappraisal*, University of Toronto Press, Toronto, 1965, pp. 369-70; G. Ross, *The Senate of Canada*, Copp Clark, Toronto, 1914, ch. 7, pp. 91-108.
11. *B.N.A. Act, 1867*, S. 50.
12. *B.N.A. Act, 1867*, S. 20.
13. *B.N.A. Act, 1867*, S. 88.
14. S.Q., 1968, C.9.
15. *The Manitoba Act*, 1870, 33 Vict., C.3.
16. *The Alberta Act*, 4-5 Ed. VII, C.3.
17. *The Saskatchewan Act*, 4-5 Ed. VII, C.42.
18. *B.N.A. Act*, 1949, 12-13 Geo. VI, C.22.
19. Johannesson v. Municipality of West St. Paul [1952], 1 S.C.R. 292. Munro v. National Capital Commission [1966], S.C.R. 663.
    Reference re Offshore Mineral Rights [1967], S.C.R. 792. Jones v. the Attorney-General of Canada et al. (1974), 45 D.L.R. (3d) 583.
20. The powers of disallowance and reservation will be discussed later.
21. *B.N.A. Act*, 1940, 3-4 Geo. VI, C.36 (U.K.).
22. *B.N.A. Act*, 1949, 13 Geo. VI, C.81 (U.K.).
23. *B.N.A. Act*, 1951, 14-15 Geo. VI, C.32 (U.K.).
24. *B.N.A. Act*, 1964, 12-13 Eliz. II, C.73 (U.K.).
25. Hodge v. The Queen (1883), 9 A.C. 117.
26. British Coal Corporation v. The King [1935], A.C. 500.
27. Naden v. the King [1926], A.C. 482.
28. British Coal Corporation v. the King, [1935], A.C. 500 at p. 519.
29. Bank of Toronto v. Lambe, 12 A.C. 575 at 581.
30. Attorney-General for Nova Scotia v. Attorney-General for Canada [1951] S.C.R. 31.
31. Re Bill 136 in the Nova Scotia Legislature, 1947, re Delegation of Legislative Jurisdiction [1948], 4 D.L.R. 1.
32. *B.N.A. Act, 1867*, S. 93(1).
33. In re George Gray (1919), 57 S.C.R. 153.
34. Gray case at p. 157.
35. Gray case at p. 157.
36. Gray case at p. 170.
37. Gray case at p. 176.
38. Gray case at p. 157.
39. R. v. Holmes [1943], 1 D.L.R. 241.
40. Reference re Regulation re Chemicals [1943], 1 D.L.R. 248.
41. Attorney-General of Canada v. Brent [1956], S.C.R. 318.
42. G.S. Rutherford, "Delegation of Legislative Power to the Lieutenant-Governors-in-Council," *Canadian Bar Review*, vol. 26, no. 3 (March 1948), p. 533.
43. Credit Foncier v. Ross [1937], 3 D.L.R. 365.
44. Hayward v. British Columbia Lower Mainland Dairy Products Board [1937], 2 W.W.R. 401.
45. Re Natural Products Marketing (B.C.) Act [1937], 4 D.L.R. 298.
46. Re Natural Products Act at p. 317.
47. Shannon v. Lower Mainland Dairy Products Board, [1938], A.C. 708.
48. Shannon case, at p. 722.
49. Switzman v. Elbling [1957], S.C.R. 285.
50. R.S.Q., 1941, C.52.
51. Switzman v. Elbling [1954], Q.B. 421.
52. Switzman v. Elbling [1957], S.C.R. 285 at p. 327.
53. Chabot v. Les Commissaires d'Ecoles de Lamorendière [1957]; Q.B. 707. See case comment on this case by F. R. Scott, "Quebec Education Act — Right of Parent over Religious Education of Child in Public School," *Canadian Bar Review*, vol. 36, no. 2 (May 1958), p. 248.
54. Chabot case at p. 722.
55. Chabot case at p. 725.
56. Regina v. Drybones (1969), 9 D.L.R. (3d) 473.
57. Attorney-General of Canada v. Lavell (1973), 38 D.L.R. (3d) 481.

Three

Subordinate Legislation and Administrative Authority

An implicit part of the concept of legislative supremacy is the right of the legislature to assign authority to other persons or bodies. In constitutional law the right of the legislature to delegate power is essential to the functioning of Canadian government. First, however, it is necessary to be clear as to what is meant by the term "delegation." One of the best judicial definitions of this term was advanced by Mr. Justice Wills in *Huth v. Clarke*,[1] where he stated, "Delegation as the word is generally used does not imply a parting with power by the person who grants the delegation, but points rather to the conferring of an authority to do things which otherwise that person would have to do himself." He continued, "It is never used by legal writers, as far as I am aware, as implying that the delegating person parts with his power in such a manner as to denude himself of his rights." Thus, delegation involves a temporary bestowing of power by the legislature, or of prerogative power by the monarchy, on a named person or body. Except for the Letters Patent of 1947, delegating the prerogative power to the Governor General, delegation in a constitutional sense means delegation by the various Canadian legislatures. It is, of course, somewhat misleading to talk in terms of temporary delegation of authority, because it is obvious that certain powers delegated to legislatively created boards and commissions, such as labour relations boards, will be exercised for very lengthy terms. The essential factor, however, is that all of these delegated powers are, in legal theory at least, subject to being withdrawn at any time by the delegator. Furthermore, the delegatees only have such powers as are given to them by statute.

The preceding chapter on the concept of supremacy of Parliament suggested some limitations on the capacity of a Canadian legislature to delegate; however, these limitations are not especially significant in terms of effective modern government. As long as Parliament retains the capacity to withdraw the authority it has assigned, the courts have upheld the placing of authority with subordinate decision-makers. The increasing use of delegation to subordinate agencies as a method of dealing with the community's problems has been the occasion for considerable expressions of fear that this represents a technique which, improperly used, could lead to a destruction of traditional constitutional values and the constitutional system itself. In the United Kingdom the most famous of these assaults was launched by Lord Hewart in his book, *The New Despotism*,[2] published in England in the late 1920's. Hewart advanced the thesis that an organized minority within the civil service was involved in what was tantamount to a conspiracy to increase their authority, through encouraging Parliament to delegate to them widespread authority. It was his view that this concentration of power was becoming increasingly uncontrolled by either Parliament or the courts, with the result that the traditional system of self-government, dominated by elected representatives, was being undermined. Lord Hewart regarded this delegation as the chief weapon bringing about the new despotism, whereas the old despotism was achieved by the Crown through the use of its prerogative power.

Canada has had its share of critics of widespread delegation, represented, for example, by the remarks of a prominent Montreal lawyer, in 1944, the late Walter S. Johnson. In an article in the *Canadian Bar Review*, entitled "The Reign of Law under an Expanding Bureaucracy,"[3] he advanced the thesis that the expanding bureaucracy being created through the use of delegation was the forerunner to the destruction of the existing constitutional order. It was his contention that the legal system was in danger of being replaced by a system whereby decision-makers operated without regard for traditional legal principles and fundamental guidelines inherited from the past. Mr. Johnson saw a threat, in that laymen, increasingly, were making legal regulations and then sitting on the board which applied these regulations to the problems brought before them. He noted a growing tendency on the part of delegatees to ignore procedure and to act without regard for precedents. One notes in both these critics a genuine concern for traditional liberties, but one cannot but sense also an underlying fear that the professional role of the lawyer and the judge is being challenged by usurpers. Mr. Johnson was considerably more justified in the comments he wrote in Canada, in 1944, than was Lord Hewart in the United Kingdom, in the late 1920's. Later there will be occasion to examine the utilization of delegated authority during war time in Canada, and this will reveal a quite perturbing use of delegation by the government, and will certainly make one read the remarks made by Mr. Johnson in a more enlightened perspective.

After the publication of Lord Hewart's book, the British government felt compelled to set up a royal commission to examine the very serious allegations which Lord Hewart had made about the role of the civil service and the dangers of delegation. The government established the Committee on Ministers' Powers,[4] which was charged with the responsibility of analysing the necessity for, and use of, delegated authority in Great Britain. Though the Committee did direct some minor criticisms at the use of delegated authority, for the most part its recommendations and conclusions constituted a rebuke to Lord Hewart. The Committee reached the conclusion that delegation was not only necessary, but inevitable, in contemporary society. They detailed the factors which had led them to this conclusion. First, they pointed out that pressure on parliamentary time makes a considerable degree of delegation essential. Furthermore, they concluded that the technicality of much of the subject matter before Parliament makes the need for decisions by experts increasingly essential. They argued that delegation is necessary to produce greater flexibility within the legislative process, while at the same time providing the opportunity for experiment. They also concluded that most new social schemes require that an authoritative person or persons be empowered to make decisions quickly, and be able to deal with unforeseen contingencies. Furthermore, the Committee felt that an emergency creates a situation in which the ponderous machinery of Parliament is not a satisfactory vehicle for rapid decision-making.

A subsequent British committee established to study administrative tribunals and enquiries, commonly known as the Franks Committee,[5] agreed with the 1932 Committee on the necessity for delegation. In the Franks Committee, however, attention was focused on the increasing tendency to delegate to administrative tribunals authority which had previously been vested in the courts. Just as the Committee on Ministers' Powers had justified a delegation of legislative powers for the previously mentioned reasons, so the Franks Committee supported the delegation of judicial powers to administrative tribunals for somewhat similar reasons. The Committee noted a number of characteristics which give administrative tribunals definite advantages over the courts. They argued that these were "cheapness, accessibility, freedom from technicality, expedition and expert knowledge of their particular subject." Though the Committee strongly expressed its preference for decision-making by the courts, if possible, it reinforced the conclusions of the 1932 Committee about the inevitability and necessity of delegation.

A variety of social factors have resulted in the shift of a considerable amount of rule-making and judicial type of authority to the governmental bureaucracy. The reasons necessitating the use of delegation outlined by the two previously mentioned committees are really only the superficial and technical ones. There are more fundamental factors which have contributed to a shifting of power away from Parliament and the courts to other sources. Government during the nineteenth century largely acted as a referee in the social, political and economic life of the nation, and its responsibilities were, accordingly, of a negative or restrictive type. It was thus relatively easy for the courts and Parliament to stand aside from the economic life of the community and draw a few prohibitory boundaries to human behaviour. The courts successfully resolved most of the disputes which arose out of economic and other matters, relying for the most part on the concepts of the common law. Popular demands, however, upon the state began to mount. For example, it readily became apparent in Canada that private industry alone could not build a powerful nation. It was accordingly necessary for the government to begin playing a role in building within Canada the paraphernalia of a modern nation. Furthermore, increased industrialization required increased state intervention, in order to regulate new conflicts within society between the owners of industry and their growing numbers of employees and consumers. Relatively little state intervention is required of an employer with ten or twenty employees, but in a situation in which an employer hires anywhere from five hundred to ten thousand workers, the whole nature of the industrial relationship between employer and employee becomes dramatically altered. Also, the Canadian people, under the influence of social philosophies brought to Canada by immigrants from Britain and Europe, tended to demand an increasingly greater share of the benefits and wealth of the community. Furthermore, private industry, as it grew larger and correspondingly more powerful, could not be left totally free to exercise its power without some restraint and control. Governments were called upon to distribute wealth, solve industrial disputes, and curb the growing might of private industrial organizations. Soon the state was required to regulate the growing power of unions, which had arisen as a counter force to the economic authority and power of the large corporations.

It is important to note the impact of new technological developments on the organization of government. New technology has meant new industry, and new industry has required governmental regulation. Trace, for example, the impact on the Canadian governmental system of the invention of radio and television. At first private radio stations operated freely in Canada, with almost no governmental regulation. This created a very difficult situation, particularly with respect to which frequencies a station would use, to name only one technical problem. Perhaps more important, however, was the fact that private radio, being operated for profit, tended to concentrate in the large centres of population, since, with relatively low transmission power, a station could reach a very wide audience. This meant that large proportions of the Canadian population, in rural areas, were totally excluded from the benefits of this new means of communication. The result was that the government was forced to appoint a royal commission charged with the task of investigating the whole problem of radio regulation in Canada. As a result of the report of this commission, a regulating body was established known as the Canadian Broadcasting Commission. This Commission was charged with the dual task of regulating private radio and creating a network of public radio stations throughout the country. One reason for the latter duty has already been mentioned, namely, that private radio stations were not serving large areas of the nation because it was not profitable for them to do so, and therefore the public demand for radio services had to be met by government action. There were other motives, however, in establishing a government radio service, mainly the desire to help promote a feeling of Canadian nationhood. Thus, the government was in the radio business for idealistic, nationalist purposes as well as to meet the legitimate demands of rural Canadians. And so, the invention of radio meant that a whole new administrative empire had to be established to meet the demands and problems created by the appearance of this new method of communication. Since it was quite obvious that Parliament itself could not lay down the innumerable regulations necessary to control radio operation and establish a public broadcasting system, it was decided to delegate authority to a number of decision-makers, who would have the day-to-day power both to regulate private radio and to operate a publicly controlled system. Parliament thus established this administrative authority and laid down the broad guidelines of its power.

A new technological development, namely, television, added to the problems of the Canadian Broadcasting Corporation, as it was now known. The Canadian Broadcasting Corporation added television services to its previous radio network. Private radio and television interests, however, protested that the body which controlled and operated the government television and radio network should not have the authority to regulate private competitors. These private interests demanded that a separate regulatory body should stand above the Canadian Broadcasting Corporation and regulate private and public television and radio. The result was the establishment of the Board of Broadcast Governors, which was charged with the task of regulating both the Canadian Broadcasting Corporation, on the one hand, and private radio and television stations on the other. This body, however, has recently been replaced by a new governmental structure called the Canadian Radio and Television Commission. Thus, the problems created by the invention of radio and television still plague government, and have resulted in a number of complicated additions to Canadian governmental machinery.

Technological change has resulted in ever-increasing specialization of function. This has, of course, meant greater productivity and industrial expansion, but has created a great many problems which must be faced by the governmental process. In a society in which the individual is trained in a very narrow specialty, he is exceptionally vulnerable to social and technological change. This has meant that in a society in which family cohesiveness has broken down and where the local community is less and less able to help its citizens, national and provincial governments must play an increasing role in protecting and retraining the worker replaced by new industrial developments. Thus, the Canadian government, like other governments, has become, in effect, an insurer of many workers against unemployment, and against dislocation of their employment due to automation and other engineering developments. This problem was met by the establishment of the Unemployment Insurance Commission by Parliament in 1940, as the result of a constitutional amendment which vested power in the national government to regulate in this field. It is of interest to note that the original attempt, in 1935, to pass federal legislation on this subject was declared *ultra vires* by the courts, thereby necessitating a formal constitutional amendment. This is the only amendment which has substantially increased the area of federal power by formally assigning to it an important area of jurisdiction. The Unemployment Insurance Commission illustrates again how technology and social change forced the government to set up new machinery, and delegate wide powers to administrative officials, in order to meet some of the problems posed by unemployment.

Within the provincial sphere the Workmen's Compensation Board is a very common example of another type of governmental insurance scheme. Essentially, the Workmen's Compensation Board is a body established by provincial legislatures to administer large sums of money to sustain men while out of work as a result of industrial accidents. The usual *modus operandi* is to require contributions to a fund by employers, and sometimes the province, with the employer's contribution varying with the number of accidents in his particular plant or business. This has had the salutary effect of encouraging safety consciousness within industry. The Workmen's Compensation Board or Commission usually pays a fixed amount per day to the worker during the period of time that he is unemployed.

This approach to solving the problem of industrial injuries is another excellent example of the failure of the traditional vehicles of the constitutional system to cope with a difficult social problem. Prior to the establishment of this type of compensation organization, it was necessary for the employee to bring an action in the courts against his employer for the injuries sustained in the course of his employment. This was an unsatisfactory method for a number of reasons. First, it was expensive and time-consuming, in that the worker had to obtain the services of a lawyer and go through the lengthy processes of a court action. It meant that the employee had to wait a substantial period of time before ultimately collecting on the judgment. Furthermore, the worker, in his action, had to establish a degree of fault on the part of his employer prior to obtaining a judgment in his favour as a result of his injury. This meant that substantial numbers of injured workmen were unable to obtain any remuneration whatsoever though they were unemployed for long periods of time. In an age when increasing numbers of the population were being employed in larger and larger industries, with no other means of sustenance except their weekly or monthly wage, some other method had to be found to solve the problem of the worker who was deprived of wages through injury.

There have, of course, been a number of other reasons why the state has had to reshape its administrative structure in order to meet social need. For example, the establishment of the Canada Wheat Board was a recognition that the state had a vested interest in the marketing of wheat, and that this could not be left uncontrolled. Similarly, the federal government has established an Atomic Energy Board in order to control uranium mining, because of the social importance of this type of product. Also, industrialization has meant a whole new series of problems involving the employer and the employee. Most of the responsibility for employer-employee relationships has tended, in Canada, to rest with the provincial legislatures, though the federal

Parliament has jurisdiction over certain inter-provincial industries, and has machinery established for the regulation of industrial relations in that area. The provinces have usually established, for their jurisdictions, labour relations boards, charged with the responsibility of deciding which unions are the appropriate bargaining agencies for the workers in a particular plant or industry. The general practice is for a labour relations board to exercise a supervisory guardianship over the voting when the workers select the union which they feel will most adequately represent them. These votes have often been the occasion for very bitter struggles between various factions in the labour movement, and have presented the labour relations boards with very difficult decisions. Furthermore, in the field of labour relations, the provinces have, through legislation, provided a whole series of techniques for the resolution of labour disputes, including conciliation officers, boards of conciliation and arbitration boards. This has meant that there is a whole network of advisory and decision-making bodies connected with helping to resolve differences between management and labour. It is an area in which feelings are extremely sensitive, and one in which these bodies are open to considerable abuse. It is a difficult field for government to regulate, and there is increasing evidence that the existing arrangements for the preservation of industrial peace are not altogether satisfactory. It thus seems that there will be considerable legislation relating to this area, probably involving new and rearranged administrative structures, in order to handle the difficult problems in this field.

Another of the chief influences bringing about recent social, political and administrative change has been the demand, by large parts of the population, for a greater share in the wealth of the national community. This is coupled with the demand that there should be a minimum standard of living beneath which no one should fall, and that the state should pass legislation and set up machinery to achieve this objective. Thus, we have witnessed, in recent years, a variety of means for redistributing wealth, and to some extent the various schemes such as unemployment insurance, workmen's compensation, and medical-health schemes, are illustrations of the implementation of that principle. The trend toward more equal distribution of wealth is most clearly reflected in the income tax system, which taxes persons of higher incomes more rigorously than those of lower income. In fact, the whole process of income tax gathering has vitally influenced governmental structure.

With the establishment of income tax in Canada, there also arose the necessity for machinery whereby the taxpayer could question whether his tax assessment was inaccurate or unlawful. Originally, the method of protest involved going to the minister responsible for income tax, namely the Minister of National Revenue, or proceeding to the Exchequer Court (now the Federal Court of Canada), under the conditions laid down by statute. It was argued that recourse to the Minister as a method of protest was unsatisfactory, in that he had a direct vested interest in the matter at hand. The result was, after considerable pressure by the legal and accounting professions, demanding that a separate governmental agency be established to hear appeals from the assessment determined by the tax authorities, that an income tax appeal board, now known as the Tax Appeal Board, was established. This body was set up to hear challenges to tax assessments, and was set up in such a way that the applicant does not have to be represented by counsel, but can appear himself or retain the services of an accountant or any other person he chooses. It is also provided that only a small fee has to be paid in order to challenge the assessment, and that this is returnable if the Board overturns the assessment. There is also provision whereby the taxpayer or the government, if unsatisfied with the decision of the Board, can proceed to the Federal Court of Canada for a further hearing. This new hearing takes the form of a trial de novo and not an appeal. The law provides that the taxpayer can ignore the Board and proceed directly to the Federal Court. This practice is increasingly being followed at the present time by large taxpayers. They feel that there is no purpose in appearing before the Board, as the case will ultimately go to this court. Furthermore, in appearing first before the Board, the taxpayer is forced to reveal his position to the government lawyers prior to going to court. Nevertheless, for the smaller taxpayer the Board serves a most useful purpose in that it is cheap, expeditious and, unless the sum is great or the principle involved is important, is usually not challenged by the government.

Every time the state has met a social need, the establishment of additional governmental machinery has usually been required. This has, accordingly, meant a shift away from Parliament and the courts towards other areas of decision-making. The time of the courts and legislatures is very limited, because their procedures have been structured so as to carefully protect and preserve important community values. Should these sometimes cumbersome procedures, which provide so much protection of liberty, be abandoned in favour of more rapid decision? In other words, is it preferable that Parliament and the courts make fewer decisions but retain the existing procedural safeguards, or should these bodies that we trust so highly make more decisions, but at the expense of their existing procedural methods? If the choice is to preserve the existing procedural methods, it is inevitable that more authority will have to be transferred to other areas of government. Then the question inevitably arises whether these other areas of government should have to follow the types of procedure utilized by the traditional institutions. This has resulted in the now frequently debated topic of the extent to which administrative authorities should judicialize their procedure. Or, to state it differently, since more and more decisions of a judicial character are being made by bodies other than the courts, should they adopt the procedures of the courts? The Franks Committee took the view that administrative tribunals should increasingly adopt proceedures similar to the courts. It was, however, because of time-consuming procedures that the courts were stripped of much of their authority, and if the administrative tribunals become as procedurally conscious as the courts, will they cease to meet the needs for which they were created? Will it mean that if they do not provide speedy, inexpensive decision-making they will, in turn, have to be replaced by other agencies of government? There are no clear-cut rules that define when decision-making should be judicialized and when it should be very informal. Undoubtedly, this will be a question for each individual agency to resolve on its own, though the courts have played a role in ascertaining that traditional procedural rights are not totally ignored by certain administrative authorities.

The same questions will have to be asked with respect to Parliament and the provincial legislatures. They have, at the present time, procedural rules which give widespread protection to the Opposition and usually allow for a maximum of debate on issues which come before them. Here again, if these rights are to be preserved, then quite obviously a great many of the detailed legislative prescriptions will have to emanate from other sources. This has, in effect, meant that Parliament has become, increasingly, a body for the debate of general issues, and that day-to-day decision-making and rule-making have fallen to other persons within the governmental structure. It is now appropriate to begin examining to whom Parliament has assigned the responsibility for passing the regulations which it has not had time, or considered appropriate, to put in the main statute. At the present time almost every statute contains some section delegating power to some agency of government. One of the great problems facing Parliament is the extent to which it should attempt to supervise the variety of agencies to which it has entrusted widespread legislative authority. The problem of parliamentary control of administrative rule-making will be examined later in this chapter.

The next question which must be faced is what kinds of power can be delegated, to whom, and under what circumstances. It is impossible to give a definitive answer to this question, as the courts have not yet drawn all the guidelines. The trend of judicial decision indicates very little restraint on the legislative right to delegate. The right to delegate is implicit in the concept of the supremacy of Parliament, a principle that has so infrequently been challenged as to still constitute a major guideline in the area of constitutional theory. Thus, it is probably safe to say that on the whole the legislature can delegate any of its powers so long as it remains within its designated legislative sphere under the terms of the British North America Act. Assuming that Parliament, or a provincial legislature, is within its field of competence as defined by the British North America Act, is there any restriction on the competency of the legislative body to delegate? One very clear restriction, already discussed, is that the federal Parliament cannot delegate to a provincial legislature, and the provincial legislatures cannot delegate to the federal Parliament. This is about the only clear-cut restriction to be found in our case law restricting the power of delegation. There is also the strong suggestion in the Gray case, also discussed previously, that the legislature cannot abdicate its legislative responsibility. This is, however, not a restriction on the right of delegation because, by definition, delegation excludes the giving away of power. Delegation always means that the delegator can withdraw the authority vested in the delegatee.

Could Parliament delegate all of its authority under the British North America Act to a subordinate body? One probable restriction on the usual right of the federal Parliament to delegate is created by the terms of Sections 53 and 54, which provide that any bill for imposing a tax shall originate in the House of Commons, and that it shall not be possible for the House of Commons to pass any bill for the raising of public revenue unless it was first recommended to the House by a message from the Governor General. Thus, any attempt to delegate total parliamentary responsibility to a subordinate body would probably fail, because, by virtue of these sections, there is in effect a veto on the right to delegate Parliament's taxing power. Subject, however, to these two exceptions, namely that Parliament cannot delegate to a provincial legislature, or delegate power to raise taxes, it is difficult to draw any other restrictions on its capacity in this area. The right of Parliament to delegate has largely gone unchallenged by the courts, except in the instance of the Nova Scotia case[6] prohibiting delegation to a legislature. Even this decision was, to a considerable extent, undermined by a decision a short time later in the Willis case,[7] which allowed both the federal and provincial legislatures the right to delegate to a provincially created body. In effect, this meant that the federal Parliament can delegate power to a creature created and established by the provincial legislature, but it cannot delegate power to the legislature itself.

This raises the question of whether there are any restraints on who can exercise delegated power. Before discussing this issue, however, a few final comments should be made with respect to the kinds of power which can be delegated. Other than the probable restriction on the right of the federal Parliament to delegate the power to tax, there seems to be no theoretical restriction on what kind of power it can delegate. The possibility that the provincial legislatures are more restricted in the kinds of power they can delegate than the federal Parliament is, has been discussed earlier in this work. As was mentioned at that time, a very small number of judges have held the view that the provincial legislatures cannot delegate the power to legislate. It is difficult to take this line of argument too seriously, particularly in view of the overwhelming trend of past events which has seen provincial legislatures delegate all types of authority to a wide variety of recipients. All of these powers have been delegated without any challenge from the courts. Thus, it is difficult to take seriously the notion that the concept of the separation of powers is a part of the fundamental guidelines of the Canadian constitution, and operates to restrict the right of either a federal Parliament or the provincial legislatures to delegate legislative or other kinds of power.

Another possible argument that might be used to suggest restrictions on a provincial legislature's right to delegate is raised by the use of the word "exclusively" in the opening paragraph of Section 92. The section provides that, "In each Province the Legislature may exclusively make Laws in relation to Matters coming within the Classes of Subjects next herein-after enumerated. . . ." Does the word "exclusively" suggest that only the legislature may make rules with respect to these subjects, and that vesting power with respect to these matters in a delegatee violates the legislature's exclusive right? In our opinion, the provincial legislatures' "exclusive" power is in relation to the federal Parliament, and not with respect to delegatees. In any event the word "exclusively" has not operated so as to restrict the provincial legislatures' power to delegate. It will be shown later that Section 96 imposes a practical, but not a theoretical, limit on the kind of power a provincial legislature can delegate.

Before analysing the question of whether there are any prohibitions with respect to who can receive delegated power, it is appropriate to examine who are the usual recipients of delegated authority in Canada. In both the federal and provincial spheres the most important delegatees are the respective cabinets in the jurisdictions concerned. It should be noted, however, that in statutes the term "Cabinet" is not used, but rather reference is made in the federal sphere to the "Governor-in-Council," and in the provincial sphere to the "Lieutenant-Governor-in-Council." In the British North America Act, 1867, Section 11 of the statute provides that, "There shall be a Council to aid and advise in the Government of Canada, to be styled the Queen's Privy Council for Canada. . . ." It is a matter of practice that all members asked to serve in the federal Cabinet are also sworn in as members of the Queen's Privy Council for Canada. Once a man is sworn into the Privy Council, he remains a member of that body for life, irrespective of whether his party continues in office or not, and irrespective of whether he holds any other elected or public office. It is, however, the conventional practice that meetings of the Privy Council are attended only by members of the federal Cabinet. It is accepted that the Cabinet is entitled to act as the Queen's Privy Council for Canada, without regard to the views of other Privy Councillors who are not at that time holding cabinet office. The legal practice is, therefore, to delegate authority to the Governor General-in-Council although, as indicated, this is in practice delegation of power to the Cabinet. Similarly, with respect to provincial government, in formal statutory terms delegation is made not to the Cabinet, but to the Lieutenant-Governor-in-Council.

Delegation has been one of the chief means whereby the federal and provincial Cabinets have gained the dominant role in Canada's governmental system. This is vividly illustrated when one examines the position of the Premiers and their Cabinets in the provinces. The legislative session for some of the smaller provinces usually lasts no longer than fourteen weeks. Even in the two largest provinces, Ontario and Quebec, the legislature usually sits only about one-half of the year. In effect, this leaves the legislature as a short-term body, appropriating funds and laying down, through statutes, the basic legal guidelines, but leaving the implementation of the legislation and the completion of much of the legislative detail to the provincial Cabinet, and the passing of regulations to other delegatees. In practice, most provincial Premiers dominate their Cabinets, particularly through their capacity to obtain the resignation of any Cabinet ministers who disagree with them. In the legislature the Premier is usually faced with a reasonably vital Opposition, which exercises a role of scrutiny and criticism, but within the private confines of the Cabinet room the Premier exercises a dominant role. Furthermore, it must be remembered that the members of the Premier's political party are very reluctant to vote against any policy of the Government in the legislature, as a defeat of Government policy means a new election. This means that Cabinet policies are rarely, particularly in recent years, defeated by a vote in the legislature. This also means that the Cabinet is thus unchallenged in its control of the legislature. In turn, the Cabinet members, though technically appointed by the Lieutenant-Governor, are in fact all named by the Premier of the day. Thus, the Cabinet is not challenged in any real sense by the legislature, and is, in turn, dominated by being largely at the mercy of the Premier. Furthermore, as has been already pointed out, because the provincial legislatures have relatively short sessions, there is real need for widespread delegation to the Cabinet. Since the Premier, if he is a man of real ability and strength (as he usually tends to be), dominates his Cabinet, he has, in fact, ultimate control over the most important part of the law-making machinery. Thus, in a very real sense, most of the power delegated to the Cabinet is, in effect, delegation to the Premier, as it is most unlikely that the Cabinet will pass an order-in-council that does not have his approval. Thus, a sequence of legal principles and conventional practices have all culminated to give Canadian provincial premiers tremendous power.

In summary, the doctrine of legislative supremacy makes the provincial legislatures virtually omnipotent within their legislative spheres. Combine this legal principle with the convention of Cabinet solidarity, and the practical requirement that party members must support the Cabinet or face an election, and the result, as has been pointed out, is a Premier who usually dominates the Cabinet and wields tremendous power. He, in effect, dominates both the Cabinet and the Legislative Assembly. Furthermore, the Lieutenant-Governor, in almost all circumstances, acts on the advice of his chief minister. Thus even more effective power is vested in the Premier. Thus the Premier in positive law has virtually no power, but through a combination of law, convention and political practice, he is, in effect, the overwhelmingly dominant figure in provincial government and politics.

In the provincial sphere it is still practicable to delegate very wide authority to a provincial Cabinet. Important, rule-making responsibility does not have to be widely dispersed throughout the provincial governmental system, whereas in Great Britain, where there is only one major government for a population of over fifty million, considerable rule-making authority is delegated to individual ministers, rather than to the entire Cabinet.

A distinction should be made in the types of power delegated by

Parliament and the legislatures of the provinces. The important power delegated is the power to make regulations. These rules, when made by the proper persons, have the same authority as if they were contained in the body of an act. However, in many instances the delegatee is only given a defined authority, involving the power to carry out the terms of the act, but not the power to make new rules in addition to those defined in the statute. The delegation of power to a wide variety of bodies and persons, to carry out specific terms of an act, is relatively common, but rule-making responsibility is usually confined to cabinets and boards and commissions.

The high-water mark in the use of delegation as a technique within the governmental process took place during the course of the First and Second World Wars. During the Second World War Canada was virtually ruled by a Cabinet dictatorship. The basis of the Cabinet's power was the War Measures Act.[8] This statute, which can be proclaimed in effect at any time by the Governor-in-Council, provides that, "The Governor in Council may do and authorize such acts and things, and make from time to time such orders and regulations, as he may by reason of the existence of real or apprehended war, invasion or insurrection deem necessary or advisable for the security, defence, peace, order and welfare of Canada. . . ." The types of regulation that can be made under this statute are then illustrated. These include, among others, the power to provide for "(a) censorship and the control and suppression of publications, writings, maps, plans, photograph, communications and means of communication; (b) arrest, detention, exclusion and deportation. . . ." Further examples of the types of specific powers mentioned in the statute include authority over harbours, ports, territorial waters, all types of transportation, trading, exportation and importation, production and manufacturing, and the control of the appropriation and disposition of property. As outlined, the foregoing specific provisions are merely illustrations of the general power, vested in the Cabinet, to make regulations for the control of the state while the War Measures Act is in effect. It is of interest to note that the Governor-in-Council has exclusive authority to proclaim the War Measures Act in effect, and any proclamation, by either Her Majesty or the Governor-in-Council is, according to Section 2 of the Act, ". . . conclusive evidence that war, invasion, or insurrection, real or apprehended, exists. . . ." Thus, by a simple unilateral act of the Cabinet, the country can replace traditional methods of constitutional practice with virtual Cabinet dictatorship. Furthermore, a provision of the War Measures Act specifically provides that no action or order taken under the authority of this statute shall be "deemed . . . an abrogation, abridgement or infringement of any right or freedom recognized by the Canadian Bill of Rights."

Lester H. Phillips, in an article published shortly after the Second World War, described how the War Measures Act was used by the Cabinet during the Second World War, to exercise incredible power with respect to the economic and political life of Canada.[9] It is important to realize the extent to which the traditional rights of Canadian citizens and residents of the country were restricted. The Commissioner of the Royal Canadian Mounted Police was appointed Registrar-General of Enemy Aliens, and was given the authority to register all citizens of countries at war with Canada, and, if necessary, subject them to internment. Furthermore, Regulation 21 allowed the Minister of Justice to detain anyone he felt might act in a manner prejudicial to the safety of the state.

Approximately twelve hundred persons were interned under the terms of Regulation 25, which provided for the detention of enemy aliens.[10] Among the Canadians detained were Adrian Arcand, the leader of the National Unity Party, a native fascist organization, along with many leaders of the Communist Party. The Communist leader, Tim Buck, and some of his aides, escaped the grasp of the authorities for two years and, after finally giving themselves up, were immediately released. The most interesting detention was that of the then Mayor of Montreal, Camillien Houde. He urged Canadians not to register with the government under the terms of the National Registration Act of 1940. This statute ordered every Canadian over the age of sixteen to register his name with the Canadian government, as a vehicle for mobilizing the manpower of the country. Mr. Houde was seized under the authority of Regulation 21 and was interned until 1944 when, upon his release, he was quickly re-elected Mayor of Montreal.

Regulation 15 authorized a federal minister to restrict the publication of any matters which, he was convinced, might be prejudicial to the efficient prosecution of the war or which threatened the safety of the state. Under the terms of this regulation a substantial number of newspapers were banned or suspended, the majority of them being Communist or foreign language newspapers. Furthermore, Regulation 39A made it an offence to print or circulate any document which might be prejudicial to recruiting, or to the safety of the state. Mr. Phillips points out that approximately three hundred persons were prosecuted under this regulation, the majority of them Communists, with the remainder being Nazi sympathizers or Witnesses of Jehovah.[11] A number of men convicted under this regulation spent fairly substantial periods of time in jail.

Regulation 39 was designed to control all statements likely to affect the war effort. At least two hundred prosecutions were launched under this regulation, mainly during the early years of the war. Penalties were varied, ranging from a few days in jail, or a small fine, up to a period of three years in the penitentiary. It is significant to note that this regulation was seldom used in the last half of the war. In fairness to the authorities, it should be remembered that, in the early years of the war, the victory of the allied forces was very much in doubt, and the insecurity of the allied participants, including Canada, must have been very great at that time. Furthermore, there was probably a good deal of uncertainty as to just how great the internal threat to the security of the state actually was. In any event the widespread use of the very great powers vested in the Governor-in-Council did achieve its object, namely, the maximum protection of internal security for the purpose of waging an effective war effort.

To the surprise of many, the Act was proclaimed by the Governor-in-Council again on October 16, 1970.[12] The occasion was the kidnapping of a Quebec cabinet minister and a British diplomat. The Governor-in-Council passed a series of regulations under the authority bestowed upon it by the Act, the essence of which involved retroactively declaring *Le Front de Libération du Québec* an illegal organization, and making membership in this organization an offence. In addition, the Government was given special powers to arrest and to search premises. The Government, however, came nowhere near to exercising the wide potential of the powers delegated by the statute. Its proclamation in peace-time, however, did result in very heated debate and criticsim from some quarters. A discussion of these questions will be left to a later part of this book which deals specifically with civil liberties. Leaving aside these three very special circumstances in which the War Measures Act has been proclaimed, there does not seem to have been any erosion of our traditional respect for civil liberties by the very tough techniques of control used during these periods. In fact, it is our view that civil liberties are more widely respected and protected now than at any other time in our history.

Thus, partly because of delegation, provincial and federal Cabinets tend to be the dominant power centres within their respective jurisdictions. As already indicated, this tends to be particularly true in the arena of provincial government, as there is often a tendency for power to be less widely shared in the provinces than it is in the federal sphere. There are probably many reasons for this, but certainly the relative brevity of the legislative session, in most provinces, is a contributing factor. Though at the federal level of government there seems little doubt that the Cabinet is the major focal point of power, nevertheless the use of power there is more carefully scrutinized by both Parliament and the press.

It is now appropriate to turn to the question of what other persons or bodies within the Canadian constitutional system frequently receive delegated power. Next to the Cabinet, the most widespread delegation of authority appears to be vested in a variety of usually semi-independent agencies, commonly called boards and tribunals. These have been established in all the provinces and in the federal sphere of government by the relevant legislatures. These bodies provide, within the governmental process, decision-makers who have some independence in relation to the Cabinet or the ordinary departmental structure. The board or commission was adopted in the United States largely as a technique for controlling natural industrial monopolies. An industry was often controlled by a single private corporation; therefore it was necessary to have some form of governmental regulation to substitute for the lack of competition. Since then boards and commissions have been set up in both Canada and the United States for a wide variety of reasons.

There are several reasons for investing power in a body that is outside the normal departmental hierarchy. First is the situation where there is a problem of judging claims as between government and an individual. In this instance the decision-maker should have some degree of independence from the minister or the deputy minister. It is also important that citizens have faith in the objectivity of the tribunal that is judging their claim. Furthermore, the board or commission has proved to be a successful vehicle for the operation of government-owned industrial and commercial enterprises. These bodies are often referred to as Crown corporations, though in their legal structure they are creatures of the legislature, just like an ordinary board or commission. For example the Canadian Broadcasting Corporation is a typical example of the use of the Crown corporation as a technique of running a commercial concern. It is quite obvious that it would be very difficult to run an organization such as a radio network as part of a regular departmental structure. The stringent job security of the ordinary departmental civil servant is just one factor which makes some special governmental structure necessary for such bodies as the Canadian Broadcasting Corporation and the National Film Board.

The semi-independent regulatory body has proved very useful in controlling large industries which do not lend themselves to ordinary departmental regulation. All the major forms of transport, including railways, airplanes, buses and trucking, are regulated by various federal and provincial boards and commissions. Another example is the Atomic Energy Control Board, established by the Atomic Energy Control Act.[13] This Board is charged with the responsibility of controlling and supervising the development and use of atomic energy in Canada. There are, of course, a great many other boards, commissions and Crown corporations that could be discussed, such as the Dominion Coal Board, the Canada Council, the Canada Wheat Board, the National Harbours Board, and the St. Lawrence Seaway Authority, to name only a few within the federal governmental structure.

Research seems only to be beginning on the actual functioning of boards and commissions in the Canadian governmental system.[14] One of the few recent examinations of boards and commissions was carried out by a committee set up by the Ontario government.[15] This committee, officially known as the Committee on the Organization of Government in Ontario, but generally referred to as the Gordon Committee, was assigned the task of making recommendations on improving the organization of government in Ontario. With respect to boards and commissions, the Gordon Committee emphasized the dangers of an improper use of this type of organization, particularly when used as a method of circumventing the traditional structure of government for a variety of improper reasons, such as evading Civil Service Commission regulations, or escaping from direct ministerial control.[16] The Committee felt that many boards and commissions are set up haphazardly, without regard to the existing structure of government. It emphasized, however, that, properly utilized, boards and commissions can play a valuable role in situations where it is inappropriate to rely on normal departmental structure. In particular, the Committee suggested that there are four major situations in which the use of the board or commission form of structure is particularly appropriate: first, when a government is taking on some new function and fairly wide discretionary powers are needed to allow the controlling body to function effectively; secondly, when the function is of a judicial nature or some special expertise is needed in making decisions; thirdly, when the function being discharged is commercial or industrial; finally, when a function cuts across existing jurisdictions or areas of responsibility.

The Committee then made a thorough examination of the various types of boards and commissions in Ontario, and grouped them into four basic categories, advisory bodies, departmental agencies, ministerial agencies and quasi-judicial agencies. It found through this grouping that there was a great dissimilarity in the power, status and role of various types of bodies designated as boards or commissions. In addition, it is interesting to note that a number of bodies, though not labelled boards or commissions, nevertheless do function as, and have a legal status similar to, agencies with those particular names. There does not seem to be any special reason why one agency is labelled a "board" and another a "commission." It might be desirable to assign the term "board" in situations where the power being exercised is of a more judicial kind. The Gordon Committee stated that many advisory bodies were without power and, accordingly, acted in a purely advisory capacity. The Committee suggested that the word "advisory" should appear in their titles, and that the term "committee" might be more appropriate when naming them. Departmental agencies were labelled as those bodies which, though made up of a separate grouping of officials, were part of the normal departmental organization. For these bodies the Committee recommended that the channel of responsibility should be through the deputy minister and then to the minister of the department concerned. Financially, they should be regarded as part of the departmental structure, and their methods of accounting and other audit provisions should be similar to those of their department. Thus, these bodies, though often called boards or commissions, are outside the usual definition of these bodies.

The final two calssifications outlined by the Gordon Committee, namely, ministerial agencies and quasi-judicial agencies, are the types of agencies normally thought of as boards and commissions. In these two groupings were bodies which had a genuinely semi-independent status, in that they were outside the normal departmental structure. These were agencies reporting to the legislature directly, through ministers of the Crown, and without any formal contact with the deputy minister or other departmental officials. This capacity to by-pass the deputy minister is the essential element which has justified the term "semi-independent" being applied to certain areas of the administrative machine. The Gordon Committee found that at the time of reporting (1959) there were thirty-two ministerial agencies and nine quasi-judicial agencies within the Ontario governmental structure. The Committee's labelling of certain bodies as "quasi-judicial" is purely arbitrary as, in terms of legal and administrative status, these bodies share an identical position with the ministerial agencies. A vital feature of the functioning of quasi-judicial agencies is that ministers of the

Crown are not responsible for individual decisions which these agencies render, whereas the minister is responsible for each decision made within his department. This means that, in cases before a quasi-judicial or ministerial agency, the body concerned is free to make whatever decision it wishes, without the immediate approval of the minister concerned. The Gordon Committee, however, stressed that, though the minister is not responsible for the individual decisions of these boards and commissions, the government and the minister of the department concerned must accept responsibility for the over-all policy an agency follows. It is because of this that the term "semi-independent" is used to describe the position of these bodies. It is, however, a very convenient arrangement in that it allows considerable freedom in decision-making within the governmental hierarchy, yet, at the same time, it is a system whereby no board can for too long follow a policy totally at variance with that of the government of the day. It is a system which appears, on the whole, to have worked satisfactorily. A later Ontario Royal Commission dealing with the above matters came to a conclusion similar to that of the Gordon Commission.[17] The Inquiry into Civil Rights (McRuer Commission) states:

> In our opinion, however, the suggestion that the doctrine of ministerial responsibility is obsolete overlooks its most important aspect. The general principle that all governmental decisions on grounds of policy should be made by Ministers, or under the control and direction of Ministers who are members of the Legislature, renders all executive action accountable to and subject to the supervision of the Legislature. The existence of the doctrine, as much as or more than its invocation in individual cases, ensures that executive action will not run counter to the will of the Legislature. This doctrine is the mechanism by which the Legislature maintains its control.

During John Diefenbaker's term as Prime Minister a dispute arose over fiscal policy between former Governor of the Bank of Canada, James Coyne, and the then Minister of Finance, Donald Fleming. This conflict was quite properly resolved with the resignation of Mr. Coyne. This was a re-affirmation of the principle referred to by the Gordon Committee, namely, that no agency of government is outside ministerial and, ultimately, legislative control, with the exception of the courts, whose role is a very special one within our constitutional system. Administrative authorities exercise only such powers as are vested in them by the legislature and, ultimately, every agency of government is, in turn, both financially and in terms of policy, responsible to the Cabinet and the appropriate legislative body.

In practice, there is considerable discrepancy in the degree to which various agencies operate subject to ministerial direction. It is in this area that there is a tremendous paucity of information about the informal and subtle day-to-day relationships between members of boards and commissions and the government of the day. Furthermore, there is a considerable difference between the legal positions of the different agencies, as regards both the areas and types of power assigned to them, and the tenure of their members and the processes by which they can be removed. Obviously, there will be a considerable discrepancy between the independence of an agency whose members have a statutory ten-year term and are removable only for misbehaviour, and a board or commission whose members have only year-to-year appointments, and are removable at the pleasure of the appropriate Cabinet. Thus, it is very difficult to generalize on the over-all position of boards and commissions within the Canadian constitutional system because, as indicated, much depends not only on the legal status of the board, but also on other informal factors, such as the personality of various participants and the role the agency has carved out for itself historically. For example, a board such as the Tax Appeal Board of Canada operates very much like a court, with any cabinet pressure very unlikely, in fact almost unthinkable. Other smaller, less prestigious bodies are probably more sensitive to government pressure, and perhaps rightly so.

A number of major questions are raised by the functionings and roles of boards and commissions in Canada. Many of these problems are common to the United States, Great Britain and Canada. First among these is one already alluded to, namely, the extent to which boards and commissions, exercising a type of authority very similar to that of the courts, should be independent of ministerial control. The Gordon Committee, as pointed out earlier, while granting the freedom of the quasi-judicial agency to make individual decisions free from ministerial supervision, denied the right of a board to depart from over-all government policy. The Franks Committee in Great Britain, however, stressed the need for greater independence of administrative tribunals from control by other parts of the administrative machine. This Committee recommended that, "tribunals should properly be regarded as machinery provided by Parliament for adjudication rather than as a part of the machinery of administration."[18] The Committee then went on to make a number of recommendations, designed to secure the independence of administrative tribunals from political supervision. Very briefly, it recommended the establishment of a council which would be charged with the responsibility of assisting, along with the Lord Chancellor, in the appointment of tribunal members, and, furthermore, the council was to exercise a watch-dog role over the functioning of administrative tribunals, and to be consulted by the government before any new tribunal was established.

In response to the Franks Committee's recommendations, Parliament passed the Tribunals and Enquiries Act.[19] This Act established a council on tribunals which, though given no effective legal powers, was to operate in an advisory capacity. Its advisory capacity included the right to make recommendations with respect to membership of tribunals. It is our view that tribunals, when exercising mainly judicial functions, should have a considerable degree of freedom but, generally speaking, it seems inappropriate to totally free administrative tribunals from over-all supervision. The recommendations of the Gordon Committee, in this respect, seem reasonable and suitable within the context of the Canadian system.

Another problem of concern in connection with boards and tribunals is the extent to which their procedures should duplicate those of the courts. Here again, there is a difference in the views put forward by the Gordon Committee and the Franks Committee. The Gordon Committee is generally reluctant to force boards and tribunals to emulate the procedural practices of the courts. The Franks Committee, on the other hand, consistent with its desire that these bodies be independent and as much like courts as possible, emphasizes that they should increasingly adopt the procedures followed by the regular judicial bodies. It is, in our view, extremely dangerous to make administrative tribunals too much like courts, because the main reasons for removing some judicial functions from the courts then will be defeated. It is, of course, difficult to generalize, but the basic problem appears to be one of balancing the slower and more orderly procedures of the courts, which, it is hoped, produce the maximum possibility of fairness, against the necessity for providing speedy relief to large numbers of applicants, with perhaps the greater probability of injustice. It is a problem to which there is no categorical and authoritative answer, but it must be reviewed from time to time by each administrative tribunal, depending on the type of work it must do, the number of applicants before it, and the time available. It is highly important that more study be done on this important problem to see if our administrative tribunals are functioning as satisfactorily as they might. (These issues are discussed, but only partially resolved, by the McRuer Commission, particularly Chapters 14 and 25 of Report I, Volume 1.)[20]

Certainly in the United States there has been a widespread criticism of the functioning of many boards and commissions. Several American writers[21] have been very critical of many recent developments in the functioning of the semi-independent regulatory bodies or, as they are often called, the headless fourth branch of government. The arguments of these critics, among others, are that these bodies no longer provide a speedy disposition of cases, and, in addition, that the process of bringing a case before them can be very costly, particularly if one wishes to maintain experienced counsel to argue one's case. Furthermore, it is argued that, often, the members of the agency lack the expert qualifications necessary to discharge their responsibilities. In the United States most appointments to these committees are for periods of only five years, and the tendency has been for men not to be reappointed, especially when a different party forms a new administration. In many instances men do not even complete their statutory five-year limit but, instead, use an appointment to a regulatory body as a stepping-stone to another career. Furthermore, it is particularly difficult to attract competent men to these positions when the tenure is so short and the possibilities of reappointment are often slight. This has often meant that the only good employment opportunity for a man who has been serving on one of these bodies is with the industry he has been regulating. As a result, it has been suggested, particularly by Professor

Schwartz, that there is a tendency for members of these agencies to render decisions which would place them in good favour with the industries which they are assigned the responsibility of controlling. For this and other reasons, there is widespread feeling that these agencies often become the protectors of the industries they are supposed to regulate. This is not entirely unnatural, as the commission is often involved in the problems of only one industry, and it is perhaps almost inevitable that it will begin to identify with that industry's problems. For example, it would not be surprising if the Interstate Commerce Commission, which has the task of regulating railways in the United States, tended to sympathize with railways in their competitive struggle with other modes of transportation, such as airlines. Furthermore, the independence of these agencies in relation to Congress is also increasingly questionable, since they are dependent on Congress for funds and, accordingly, their operation has been influenced by congressional committees. Thus, the history of semi-independent regulatory bodies in the United States has not been an altogether happy one, and there is an obvious need for a variety of changes in such areas as organization, procedure, and terms of appointment.

Are we in Canada plagued by the same problems with respect to our regulatory boards and commissions as the United States? As already pointed out, there is unfortunately a great dearth of research on the functioning of our boards and commissions, so that it is virtually impossible to reach definite conclusions. It is our impression, however, that boards and commissions in Canada do not seem to be afflicted by the same difficulties, and certainly have not been publicly criticized as their counterparts in the United States have been. Perhaps one salient reason for this is the fact that most of our important boards and commissions, at least at the federal level, have members whose tenure is usually ten years. Removal of board members is very rare, and the general pattern seems to be to reappoint a man to a commission after the completion of his term. Perhaps another reason why Canadian administrative agencies have been less frequently under attack is that the problems they have had to cope with have not been as complex as those in the more industrialized United States. Perhaps it is only a question of time until the industrial problems of the United States catch up with us and, accordingly, create for our boards and commissions problems similar to those of the United States. It is our suspicion, however, that the length of tenure of our board members is going to be an important factor in meeting many of the problems that have evolved in the United States. Length of tenure enables a man to become more expert in his field. It also allows board members to evolve a greater sense of independence and, accordingly, tends to increase confidence in them on the part of both industry and government. Certainly, most of the criticisms of the American agencies seem to centre on the very poor quality of men appointed to serve as members of the commissions concerned. Thus it seems clear that we can avoid many of the problems of American regulatory bodies if we continue to appoint to our boards high calibre personnel, guaranteeing them a sustained tenure, and as high a degree of independence as possible, while not forgetting the over-all principle that the general policy of every board or commission must ultimately conform to that of the government.

Authority has, by virtue of federal and provincial statutes, been delegated to a wide variety of persons and organizations. In addition to the delegation of power to the respective Cabinets, boards and commissions of both the federal and provincial governments, there has been some delegation of authority to individual Cabinet ministers. Canadian Cabinet ministers, however, are not usually given powers so often, nor are the powers so important as those delegated to their counterparts in Great Britain. As already suggested, this is largely due to the fact that a unitary government places unusual stress on the single Parliament and single Cabinet which must run the entire country. The division of legislative power in Canada means that delegated authority can still be vested generally, in Cabinets rather than individual ministers. It is our impression that it is more usual for the federal Parliament to delegate authority to a minister than it is for a provincial legislature. This is probably explained by the fact that the provincial Cabinet, having a smaller number of matters to deal with, can still exercise the main rule-making role within its jurisdiction. It is interesting to note that the McRuer Commission recommends that the authority to make legislative regulations be delegated only to the Lieutenant-Governor-in-Council, or that this body at least approve legislative regulations made by other subordinate bodies.

Distinction, thus, must be made between different degrees of delegated power. It is quite common to vest in both Cabinets, and boards and commissions the right to make regulations which have the same force and effect as if they were contained in a statute. It is very rare to see rule-making authority vested in ministers of the Crown. Instead, one tends to see a delegation of authority which allows a minister to carry out the terms of an act; for example, in the Post Office Act it is provided that, "Subject to this Act, the Postmaster-General shall administer, superintend and manage the Post Office, and without restricting the generality of the foregoing may . . ."[22] and there then follows a long list of powers. The right to make regulations is not included among these powers. Presumably, however, one might argue that the right to administer and superintend a Post Office involves the right to issue orders to the staff, which is tantamount to issuing regulations under the Act. Nevertheless, this is, in substance, a power different from the right to make regulations which have the same effect as if they were in the statute itself. It is interesting to note that when the first edition of this book was published, the Pest Control Products Act provided that: "the Minister may make regulations (a) prescribing for the purposes of this Act the nomenclature of every form of plant and animal life that shall be deemed to be pests."[23] This Act has since been amended to read: "The Governor in Council may make regulations. . . ."[24] Thus, it is becoming rare to find examples of rule-making, as distinct from purely administrative, powers being delegated to individual ministers.

It is quite common to have included in federal and provincial statutes the vesting of responsibilities in officials who are part of the ordinary governmental structure. It is, however, not usual practice for Parliament or the legislature to vest in departmental officials the right to make regulations. Usually, when vesting authority in someone other than the minister, the statute provides that this particular official has certain specific duties assigned to him. For example, in the federal Public Works Act it is provided in Section 8, "The Chief Engineer or the Chief Architect shall (a) prepare maps, plans and estimates for all public works that are about to be constructed, altered or repaired."[25] After a number of specific responsibilities assigned to him are listed, there follows the general statement that he shall "(d) generally advise the Minister on all engineering or architectural questions affecting any public work." Similarly, one finds in the R.C.M.P. Act the following section: "5. The Governor in Council may appoint an officer to be known as the Commissioner of the Royal Canadian Mounted Police who, under the direction of the Minister, has the control and management of the force and all matters connected therewith."[26] Here, the Commissioner is given the power to lay down rules binding on the internal members of the Force, but has no authority to make regulations binding on the general public. It is important to note this distinction between assigning to an official the responsibility for carrying out duties defined by statute, and assigning to a delegatee the right to make regulations which are as binding on the general public as if they were contained in the statute itself.

Cabinet ministers, boards and commissions, and specified government officials are not the only recipients of delegated power in Canada. For example, it is not uncommon to delegate authority to judges to make rules governing procedure in civil matters. The judges of the Supreme Court of Canada, in Section 103 of the Supreme Court Act, are given authority to lay down their rules of procedure. The statute provides that the "judges of the Supreme Court, or any five of them, may make general rules and orders (a) for regulating the procedure of and in the Supreme Court and the bringing of cases before it from courts, appeal from or otherwise, and for the effectual execution and working of this Act, and the attainment of the intention and the objects thereof. . . ."[27]

Another area in which one often sees provincial and federal parliaments delegating authority is that which relates to the internal management of certain professions. In the provincial sphere, one sees a whole series of statutes setting up and delegating authority to various bodies charged with the responsibility for the regulating of provincial professional groups.[28]

It is now appropriate to examine whether there are any prohibitions with respect to who can receive delegated power. In other words, are there certain persons in whom, or bodies in which, the provincial legislatures or the federal Parliament cannot delegate authority?

The first clear-cut restriction on who or what can receive delegated power is one that has already been mentioned several times previously in this work. This is the rule that the federal Parliament and a provincial legislature cannot delegate power to each other. This decision was handed down by the Supreme Court of Canada in the Nova Scotia case.[29] For reasons outlined earlier in this book, it is our view that this decision was inconsistent with the basic principles of Anglo-Canadian constitutional law and, in addition, was an undesirable restriction on legislative power in terms of national policy. The decision certainly appears particularly questionable when, a very short time after it was handed down, the Supreme Court of Canada allowed a scheme whereby the federal Parliament and a provincial legislature delegated authority to a board created by the legislature of Prince Edward Island.[30]

In the Nova Scotia case, the court was obviously frightened by the implications of the inter-delegation scheme which had been brought before it. Essentially, the courts seemed to think that this would be a back door method of destroying the division of legislative powers outlined in the British North America Act. It seemed to be assumed throughout this case that what was involved was an abdication of power by one legislative jurisdiction in favour of another. Only Mr. Justice Doull of the Nova Scotia Court of Appeal stressed that by definition, delegation did not mean abdication of power by the delegator.

In addition, it strikes us that the Nova Scotia decision might be circumvented by a number of methods. For example, what would a court say if the delegation was made by the federal Parliament to a list of named people? This list of named people could, incidentally, all be members of a provincial legislature. In that situation one could argue that this was not delegation to a provincial legislature, but to a group of specified individuals, which, in our view, is perfectly permissible within the Canadian constitutional system. In addition, the arguments of the Supreme Court of Canada in the Willis case could be advanced to support the validity of this delegation. In the Willis case, some of the Supreme Court of Canada judges said that if, by coincidence, the federal Parliament happened to delegate authority to the five members of a provincial marketing board, this coincidence should not spoil the validity of the delegation. Similarly, it is arguable that the delegation to twenty-four named persons who, by coincidence, also happened to be members of the Prince Edward Island legislature should be upheld on the same principles as those that governed the decision in the Willis case. It is unlikely that a subterfuge of this type would be resorted to, but it demonstrates that the decision in the Nova Scotia case would not be an impossible one to circumvent, if the political decision-makers were determined to achieve inter-delegation in fact, if not in theory.

Section 96 of the British North America Act has imposed a practical, if not theoretical, restriction on the right of provincial legislatures to delegate to certain types of persons. Section 96 provides that the judges of the superior, district and county courts of each province shall be appointed by the Governor General. For example, in the case of *Toronto v. York Township et al.*, the Ontario Court of Appeal[31] and Privy Council[32] both held that the conferring upon the Ontario Municipal Board, by the provincial legislature, of the power to construe the terms of a contract was *ultra vires.* The argument of both these courts was that the power to interpret contracts has traditionally been a function of superior and county courts and, therefore, though the law relating to contracts comes within the purview of the provincial legislature as being part of property and civil rights, the legislature cannot delegate its authority in this area to persons not nominated by the Governor-General. The court argued that this was tantamount to violating the terms of Section 96. Assume, however, that the members of the Ontario Municipal Board had been named by the Governor General. Would this have meant that the delegation of authority to interpret contracts was valid, or would it have meant that the delegation would only be valid if the Governor General had specifically appointed the delegatees as Section 96 court judges? There is, within the law, no answer to this question. However, if nomination by the Governor General alone does not satisfy the requirements of the courts, as outlined in the York Township case, then it must be assumed that authority over certain subjects within provincial jurisdiction cannot be delegated by the provincial legislatures to bodies of their own creation and appointment. That is to say, if it is found that a type of power was similar to that traditionally exercised by Section 96 judges then, if the York Township decision is correct, perhaps no delegation of this power can be made by the provincial legislature unless it is made to a member of the judiciary. Assume, however, that the nomination is made by the Governor General, but the delegatee is not named as a member of the judiciary, does this render the delegation invalid? If it does, that means that there is an area of power which can only be delegated by the provincial legislature to specific persons, namely district, superior and county court judges, who have been appointed by the Governor General. It is our view that, with certain Section 96 functions, it is sufficient that the nomination be made by the Governor General, without naming the nominee as a judge. If this assumption is correct, then it imposes, as already suggested, a practical, if not theoretical, limit on the provincial legislature in the area of delegation.

In view of the foregoing situation it is quite understandable why the courts have been reluctant to strike down the validity of provincial delegation by the use of the Section 96 argument. As pointed out, this would lead, in effect, to prohibiting the provincial legislature from delegating important areas of power, if the function of district, county and superior courts was to be interpreted in its broadest sense. Since the first edition of this book, however, there have been a few relatively insignificant cases wherein the courts have utilized the section 96 argument to declare *ultra vires* delegation by the provincial legislatures to provincial appointees.

The leading case dealing with Section 96, the *Labour Relations Board of Saskatchewan v. John East Ironworks Ltd.*,[33] is an excellent example of the refusal of the courts, in this case the Privy Council, to accept Section 96 as a basis for striking down delegation to a provincially created and appointed body. In the John East Ironworks case it was argued before the court that the Labour Relations Board, having been assigned the power to force an employer to reinstate any employee discharged in violation of the Labour Relations statute, and to order the employer to compensate the employee for money lost as a result of an illegal discharge, was exercising the function of a superior, district or county court. The Privy Council, in a long judgment, rejected this argument. The Judicial Committee held that the Board was essentially involved in the promotion of industrial peace, and that the powers just referred to were merely incidental to its main purpose. In addition, they went on to show a number of ways in which the Board differed from a superior court, thereby refusing to accept the argument of counsel that there was any violation of Section 96.

Section 96 has been used to challenge the validity of workmen's compensation commissions in at least two provinces. The argument has been, in both instances, that the workmen's compensation boards were exercising the functions of Section 96 courts and, since board members were appointed by the provincial authorities, their exercise of authority was illegal. This argument was quickly dismissed by the Court of Appeal of British Columbia in the case of *Farrell et al. v. Workmen's Compensation Board*,[34] and was not used at the Supreme Court of Canada level.[35] In the *Attorney-General of Quebec v. Slanec and Grimstead*,[36] a good deal of attention was devoted to the Section 96 argument, but the court concluded that the functions of the Quebec Workmen's Compensation Commission were essentially administrative rather than judicial, and therefore the terms of Section 96 were inapplicable. Similarly, the argument that the provincial appointment of members of the Quebec Public Service Commission was a violation of Section 96 was struck down by the Privy Council in the decision of *O. Martineau & Sons Ltd. v. Montreal*.[37] The court in this case examined the matter in historical perspective and found that the superior courts of the province had never exercised the kind of responsibilities vested in the Quebec Public Service Commission. All of these cases are illustrative of the reluctance of the courts to allow the use of Section 96 as a technique for invalidating established and important parts of provincial administrative machinery. It is essential, when assigning power in a constitution to a legislature, that the legislature be given the power to delegate responsibility to appropriate delegatees.

Other than the areas mentioned above, there appear to be no other restrictions on the right of federal and provincial legislatures to delegate. As was indicated earlier in this chapter, a few attempts were made, in isolated cases, to suggest that the doctrine of the separation of powers was part of the Canadian constitutional structure and that one branch of government, namely the legislature, was not entitled to delegate its functions to other parts of the governmental structure. From the relatively few decisions on this subject it is our conclusion that these decisions are rare and wrong. The courts have upheld Parliament's and the provincial legislatures' right to delegate a broad assortment of powers to different individuals and bodies. Furthermore, if the legislature is quite clear in its language, the courts have been willing to uphold substantial re-delegation of authority from a delegatee to a sub-delegatee. It is difficult to be definitive on this subject, because of the relatively few decisions dealing with the outer limits of delegation. Except during war time, the federal and provincial legislatures have been reasonably discreet in the use of delegation, and have thus, perhaps, limited the amount of litigation challenging the legislative right in this area. Undoubtedly, the doctrine of the supremacy of the legislature has been another factor in making the courts hesitant to challenge the right of the legislature to delegate. Furthermore, it is, in our view, undesirable that the right of delegation should be seriously restricted. Surely, it is for the legislature to decide when powers should be vested in administrative hands. If the legislators are careful to review the use of delegated authority by delegatees and are reasonably cautious about the types of power delegated, then the primary responsibility in this area should rest with them. The courts have played a leading role in controlling the action of delegatees who have stepped outside the authority vested in them, but, as already pointed out, they have shown very little desire to restrict the right of delegation itself.

REFERENCES

1. *Huth v. Clarke* (1890), 25 Q.B.D. 381, at p. 395.
2. G. Hewart, *The New Despotism*, E. Benn, London, 1929.
3. W.S. Johnson, "The Reign of Law Under an Expanding Bureaucracy," *Canadian Bar Review*, vol. 22, no. 4 (April 1944). p. 380.
4. *Report of the Committee on Ministers' Powers*, Cmd. 4060, H.M.S.O., London, 1932, rep. 1956.
5. *Report of the Committee on Administrative Tribunals and Enquiries*, Cmd. 218, H.M.S.O., London, 1957, reprinted 1958 (hereinafter referred to as the Franks Report).
6. See f.n. 30, ch. 2.
7. *Prince Edward Island Potato Marketing Board v. Willis and Attorney-General of Canada* [1952], 4 D.L.R. 146.
8. R.S.C., 1970, C.W-2.
9. L. H. Phillips, "Canada's Internal Security," *Canadian Journal of Economics and Political Science*, vol. 12, no. 1 (February 1946), p. 18.
10. L. H. Phillips, "Canada's Internal Security," p. 27.
11. L. H. Phillips, "Canada's Internal Security," p. 23.
12. SOR/70-443.
13. R.S.C., 1970, C.A-19.
14. See, for example, C. A. Ashley and R. G. H. Smails, *Canadian Crown Corporations*, Macmillan of Canada, Toronto, 1965; T. Willis (ed.), Canadian Boards at Work, Macmillan of Canada, Toronto, 1941.
15. *Report of the Committee on the Organization of Government in Ontario*, Toronto, September 1959 (hereinafter referred to as the Gordon Report).
16. Gordon Report, ch. 4, pp. 48-82.
17. *Royal Commission Enquiry into Civil Rights*, Report no. 1, vol. 1, Queen's Printer, Ontario, 1968, p. 126.
18. Franks Report, para. 40, p. 9.
19. 6-7 Eliz. II, C.66 (U.K.).
20. Royal Commission Enquiry into Civil Rights, Report no. 1, vol. 1, Queen's Printer, Ontario, 1968, chs. 14 to 25.
21. B. Schwartz, *The Professor and the Commissions*, Knopf, New York, 1959. J. M. Landis, "The Administrative Process: The Third Decade," *American Bar Association Journal*, February 1961, p. 35. Stanley Gerwitz, "The Paradoxes of Government

by Regulation," an unpublished paper delivered at the third annual Air Transport Conference held in September 1963.

22. *R.S.C., 1970,* C.P-14, S. 5(1).
23. *R.S.C., 1952,* C.209, S. 12.
24. *R.S.C., 1970,* C.P-10, S. 5.
25. *R.S.C., 1970,* C.P-38, S. 8.
26. *R.S.C., 1970,* C.R-9, S. 5.
27. *R.S.C., 1970,* C.S-19, S. 103.
28. For example, in British Columbia, the Dentistry Act establishes the College of Dentistry and then vests regulatory power in the College. *R.S.B.C., 1960,* C.99.
29. See f.n. 30, ch. 2.
30. See f.n. 7, above.
31. *Toronto v. York Township et al.* [1937], 1 D.L.R. 175.
32. *Toronto v. York Township et al.* [1938], 1 D.L.R. 593.
33. *Labour Relations Board of Saskatchewan v. John East Ironworks Ltd.* [1948], 1 D.C.R. 771.
34. *Farrell et al. v. Workmen's Compensation Board* (1961), 26 D.L.R. (2d) 185.
35. *Farrell et al. v. Workmen's Compensation Board and Attorney-General of British Columbia* (1962), 31 D.L.R. (2d) 179
36. *Attorney-General of Quebec v. Slanec and Grimstead* [1933], 2 D.L.R. 289.
37. *O. Martineau and Sons Ltd. v. Montreal* [1932], 1 D.L.R. 353.

Four

The Crown and Prerogative Power in Canada

The British North America Act, in Section 9, provides that, "The Executive Government and authority of and over Canada is hereby declared to continue and be vested in the Queen." The fact that Canada is a monarchy has important legal and other ramifications often not fully appreciated by the population of the country. First, there is vested in the monarch a series of powers and rights, usually referred to as the "prerogative," which are exercised by the monarch, or the monarch's representatives, independent of and apart from statute. This prerogative power is, in effect, the residue of special rights, privileges and powers left to the monarch from historical times. It is true that many of these powers are exercised usually on the advice of the Prime Minister or other members of the Cabinet, but, at the same time, the fact that the federal and provincial governments are carried on in the name of the monarch allows these governments the protection of the special privileges accorded to the monarch. In a narrow legal sense government in Canada is very much the Queen's government. For example, we speak of the Queen's judges. Certain lawyers are given the title of Queen's Counsel by virtue of an exercise of the royal prerogative on the part of the government. State-owned lands are called Crown lands, and public corporations are Crown corporations. Commissioned officers in the Armed Forces are said to have the Queen's commission. Section 17 of the British North America Act provides that, "There shall be One Parliament for Canada, consisting of the Queen, an Upper House styled the Senate, and the House of Commons." We note that all prosecutions in the criminal courts are taken in the name of the monarch, and, similarly, when the government is involved in a lawsuit it is usually referred to as "the Queen." Though Her Majesty might be called upon by her Canadian ministers to perform certain functions in her capacity as Queen of Canada, the majority of the monarchical duties are performed, in right of Canada, by the Governor General, and, in right of the provinces, by a Lieutenant-Governor for each province. The Governor General and the Lieutenant-Governors are in no respects representatives of the British government, but are in fact representatives of the monarch.

There are many who would argue that any time spent on the office of either Governor General or Lieutenant-Governor is simply wasted, and that a constitutionalist would be well advised to either ignore or spend little time on this subject. In terms of power the role of the Governor General or the provincial Lieutenant-Governor is indeed a limited one. Although the formal legal powers vested in both of these offices is very great, it is usually recognized that the majority of these powers are, in almost all cases, exercised upon the advice of either the federal Prime Minister or a provincial Premier. During this analysis of the roles of the Governor General and the Lieutenant-Governors, there will be an attempt to show that it would be undesirable to regard as totally extinguished potentially independent decision-making by any of the Queen's representatives in Canada. The powerful position of the Cabinet has been stressed in this work, especially the political strength of the federal Prime Minister and the provincial Premiers. To cast aside without question any independent role whatsoever for either the Governor General or the Lieutenant-Governors is to remove one of the few — and, in many cases, the only — possible restraints on the actions of the Prime Minister or a provincial Premier.

While recognizing that ultimate authority must always rest in some decision-maker, one must at the same time recognize that excessive authority placed in a few hands without recourse to other sources of power is extremely dangerous. In Canada, we have perhaps reached this very dangerous position, and those persons who have glibly suggested that the Governor General and provincial Lieutenant-Governors should be purely ceremonial figures have done the cause of countervailing power a considerable disservice. This does not mean that we should establish the Governor General or the Lieutenant-Governors as rivals to the Prime Minister or Premiers, or that there should be allowed a very widespread independent use of prerogative or statutory power by the Governor General or the Lieutenant-Governors. It is in accordance with our tradition that these office-holders will almost always act on the advice of their chief advisers at the federal and provincial level. This is the way it is, and this is the way it should be. The Governor General and the Lieutenant-Governors are appointees, and elected officials should play the predominant role in our governmental and constitutional system. This is not to say, however, that just because these men are appointees they should have no power whatever. We have ample precedents, including the judiciary and civil service, for allowing wide power to appointed officers. There are special circumstances, reasonably well defined by previous practice, where the Queen's representatives should be allowed to protect the public from certain recommendations by the Prime Ministers or Premiers and their Cabinets. Later in this chapter we shall attempt to point out situations in which the personal judgment and action of the Governor General or the Lieutenant-Governors would be both constitutionally permissible and desirable. Before discussing these instances, however, it is appropriate to examine in some detail the offices of Governor General and Lieutenant-Governor.

The office of Governor General, in Canada, is created not by statute, but by Letters Patent emanating from the monarch. The most recent Letters Patent were issued in October 1947, and provide that, "There shall be a Governor-General and Commander-in-Chief in and over Canada, and appointments to the Office of Governor-General and Commander-in-Chief in and over Canada shall be made by Commission under Our Great Seal of Canada." Thus, the office of Governor General is constituted by direct order of the monarch, as an exercise of the monarch's prerogative powers.

The Letters Patent not only create the office of Governor General, but delegate to the Governor General the monarch's prerogative powers. The earlier Letters Patent merely vested certain prerogative powers in the Governor General, with the remainder resting with the monarch. It must be remembered, however, that even though these powers remained with the monarch, they were exercised only on the advice of his or her Canadian ministers. Until 1947, the Letters Patent were always accompanied by instructions from the monarch on how the prerogative powers were to be exercised. In 1947, not only was there a deletion of instructions, but the Letters Patent of that year delegated all of the monarch's lawful authority with respect to Canada. The Letters Patent provide that, "we do hereby authorize and empower Our Governor-General, with the advice of Our Privy Council for Canada or any members thereof or individually, as the case requires, to exercise all powers and authorities lawfully belonging to Us in respect of Canada. . . ." The Letters Patent then outline a number of illustrations of the power vested by the monarch in the Governor General. For example, in Part IV, the Governor General is given the right to appoint on behalf of the monarch, "Judges, Commissioners, Justices of the Peace, and other necessary Officers (including diplomatic and consular officers) and Ministers of Canada, as may be lawfully constituted or appointed by Us." This clause illustrates some of the important legal powers vested in the Governor General, in that many of the most important decision-makers within the state are technically appointed by him. One does not, however, need a very sophisticated knowledge of Canadian constitutionalism to understand that all of these appointments are made by the Governor General on the advice of either the Prime Minister or the entire Cabinet. Further on in this chapter there is an outline of a minute of the Privy Council, indicating which of the legal powers of the Governor General are exercisable only on the advice of the Prime Minister.

There are a number of other powers spelled out in the Letters Patent, connected with the office of Governor General. Part V authorizes him to "remove from his office, or to suspend from the exercise of the same, any person exercising any office within Canada, under or by virtue of any Commission or Warrant granted, or which may be granted, by Us in Our name or under Our authority." Presumably this section allows the Governor General to remove Cabinet ministers from office. It is obvious that a large number of important officials within the state could technically be removed by the Governor-General, acting on the advice of the Prime Minister. It is necessary, however, to keep in mind that, with respect to federally appointed judges, the method of their removal is determined by statute. Nevertheless, the right to remove Cabinet ministers is a very important power vested in the Governor General and, by virtue of convention, it places the Prime Minister in a powerful position as regards controlling his Cabinet.

Part VI of the Letters Patent vests a very important and most controversial power in the Governor General. It provides that the Governor General will have all the traditional powers of the monarch, "in respect of summoning, proroguing or dissolving the Parliament of Canada." It was in the exercise of the power of dissolution that Canada had its only major political and constitutional crisis centring on the office of the Governor General. Further on, we shall analyse this crisis and attempt to ascertain whether it resolved the constitutional position of the Governor General in relation to his right to dissolve Parliament.

Part XII of the Letters Patent vests in the Governor General the right to pardon and reprieve persons convicted of criminal offences. It is notable, however, that this part specifically spells out the conventional role of the Cabinet with respect to the Governor General's actions. It provides that the "Governor-General shall not pardon or reprieve any such offender without first receiving in capital cases the advice of Our Privy Council for Canada and, in other cases, the advice of one at least of his Ministers." Thus, since the only active part of the Privy Council is the Cabinet, this, in effect, means that no capital cases can be commuted to life imprisonment without a decision by the Cabinet.

Thus, it is probably correct to conclude that, even though some functions can still be exercised by the monarch on the advice of the Canadian Cabinet or Prime Minister, all of these can now be performed by the Governor General. At the time of the issuance of the 1947 Letters Patent, however, the then Prime Minister, Louis St. Laurent, indicated that the Cabinet would still feel free to call upon the monarch, acting as the King or Queen of Canada, to perform certain functions, such as the naming of ambassadors or the declaration of war and peace.

It is often forgotten that the prerogative not only confers upon the monarch or the Governor General the legal power to make decisions, but also confers certain special privileges and immunities upon the state. These special rights accorded the monarch, as a legal person, accrue to the Queen's government both in right of Canada, and in right of each province, except to the extent that they have been abrogated by statute. Let us examine more fully some of the special privileges which the monarch possesses as a legal person.

Under the common law, the monarch is entitled to a number of special prerogatives and privileges: for example, the monarch is not liable in tort, either personally or as a result of acts done by agents of Her Majesty. This common law prerogative right of the monarch has been removed to a large extent in Great Britain and Canada, by virtue of statute.[1] However, some provinces continue to enjoy this immunity from suit, by virtue of the Crown prerogative attaching to the Lieutenant-Governor, though often this right is waived by representatives of the provincial governments. There are a number of other prerogative rules that operate to benefit the government concerned. For example, Her Majesty is entitled to property that would otherwise be ownerless. Similarly, Her Majesty is entitled to a priority in the payment of debts, over other creditors. This means, with respect to the first of the two rules that when a person dies intestate and there is no one entitled by law to receive the property, it automatically accrues to the government. There are a number of prerogatives of a parliamentary nature vested in Her Majesty and exercisable by her representative, be it the Governor General or a Lieutenant-Governor. The power to prorogue and dissolve Parliament is one of these powers, and it is referred to in the Letters Patent. Traditionally, the royal prerogative allowed the monarch to establish courts of common law, but in view of the specific provisions of the British North America Act surrounding the establishment of courts, this prerogative power no longer exists in Canada. Among the more important rights of the monarch, now exercisable by the Governor General by virtue of the 1947 Letters Patent, are those relating to external affairs. Her Majesty, for example, is capable of entering into treaties on behalf of Canada, or of declaring war and peace, or of naming ambassadors, following always, of course, the advice of her Canadian ministers. By virtue of the Letters Patent, 1947, these prerogative powers can now be carried out by the Governor General, acting on the advice of the Canadian Cabinet. It is accepted by the courts that Her Majesty, and therefore the government, is not bound by statute unless specifically named in the statute.

It is essential, however, to underline the fact that none of these prerogative powers is entrenched, in the sense that they cannot be altered or removed. One need only examine the traditional common law prerogative exempting Her Majesty from suit. This, in effect, meant that one could sue a servant of the Crown personally for illegal acts, but one could not utilize the law of agency to make the employer (in this case the government) responsible. Both Great Britain and the Canadian government have seen fit, by virtue of statute, to legislate away this prerogative right. Similarly, any one of the prerogative rights could be changed by an appropriate statute. If a prerogative was abolished by statute, then it could never be restored in its pure form. It is true that the monarch, or the monarch's representative, could be given special powers by statute, but this would amount to delegation and would no longer constitute an exercise of the prerogative.[2]

In addition to his prerogative powers, the Governor General has certain responsibilities assigned to him by the terms of the British North America Act. Section 11 provides for the establishment of a Privy Council to aid and advise in the government of Canada, and at the same time provides that the members of this Privy Council shall be "chosen and summoned by the Governor-General."[3] The section also provides that they may be removed by the Governor General. As has been already frequently mentioned, virtually all of the powers of the Governor General are exercised upon the advice of the Prime Minister. Thus, the Governor General only summons persons to be members of the Privy Council upon the advice of the Prime Minister and, similarly, would only remove them upon the advice of the Prime Minister. Once again, this underlines the tremendously powerful position of the Prime Minister in the Canadian system, in that the terms of Section 11, combined with convention, allow him to remove any member of his Cabinet at any time. In actual fact, however, this technique would probably not be used; instead, the Prime Minister would ask for the resignation of the minister concerned.

There are a number of other important provisions in the British North America Act relating to the office of Governor General. Section 24 of the British North America Act vests in the Governor General the power to make appointments to the Senate of Canada. Section 34 gives him the power to appoint a senator to be Speaker of the Senate, and also the right to remove him. Section 54 provides that the House of Commons cannot pass any measure involving the appropriation of public funds, without this having first been recommended to the House by a message from the Governor General. This, in effect, is a technique whereby the Cabinet controls all bills involving the expenditure of public funds.

Section 55 vests in the Governor General the power to assent or withhold assent to bills, or to reserve them for the pleasure of the monarch. In contemporary Canada it would, of course, be unthinkable for the Governor General to reserve any bill for the pleasure of the monarch. Similarly, it is very difficult to envisage a situation in which the Governor General would withhold his assent to a bill passed through the Senate and the House of Commons. One should, however, not be too glib in totally dismissing this right on the part of the Governor General. For example, there may arise a serious enough situation whereby what is in effect a veto power might appropriately be used. For example, if a bill proposed to abolish the Opposition, surely the Governor General should be allowed to assert independently his legal right. The counter-argument to this proposition is that, if such a situation ever arose, we would be in a political environment so different from the current one that the threat of a Governor General's veto would be ineffective. Therefore, one can probably say that, assuming that the general political system as we know it continues, it is extremely unlikely that we shall ever see an instance in which the Governor General unilaterally refuses to give his assent to a bill.

Section 96 of the Act vests in the Governor General the power to appoint judges of the superior, district and county courts in Canada.[4] At the same time the Act provides that the Governor General has the power to remove superior court judges, but only after an address of the Senate and House of Commons. With respect to the power of appointing judges, as would be expected, this power is exercised only upon the advice of the Cabinet and, in particular, the Prime Minister and Minister of Justice.

One occasion on which the Governor General has involved himself in a definitely major political controversy centred on the conventional right of the Governor General to refuse to dissolve the House of Commons in order that there could be a general election. There was, of course, no doubt that in positive law this power was vested in him, by virtue of the Letters Patent and Section 50 of the British North America Act. It is not our intention to outline the so-called Byng crisis in excessive detail, as this has been done very ably by a number of writers, particularly Dr. Eugene A. Forsey.[5] The Prime Minister, subsequent to the 1921 election, was the leader of the Liberal Party, Mr. Mackenzie King. On September 5, 1925, Mr. King asked for, and received, a dissolution of Parliament by the Governor General. The results of the election, on October 29, 1925, produced a House of 101 Liberals, 116 Conservatives and 24 Progressives, plus assorted Independents. Mr. King, however, despite having fewer seats than the Conservative Party, chose to remain in office and meet the House. He continued in office by virtue of the support of the 24 Progressives who had won seats in the election. By June, the Government was faced with a serious Customs scandal and a vote of censure was before the House. During the weekend of June 26-27 Mr. King asked for a dissolution of the House. The Governor General, Lord Byng, refused to grant the dissolution; King thereupon followed the unusual course of immediately handing in his resignation. Mr. King argued that he believed he was entitled, by convention, to dissolution, on the grounds that the Governor General was not entitled to exercise any option in this matter.

The Governor General then asked Arthur Meighen if he would form a Government, which Mr. Meighen agreed to do. Politically, this was rather foolish, in view of the fact that, since the King Government had been faced with a serious scandal, there was a very strong possibility that it would have been defeated at a general election if a dissolution had been granted. Meighen's biographer, Roger Graham, argues that, as a matter of honour, Mr. Meighen thought that he must try to form a Government to help justify the position taken by Lord Byng.[6] After three days in office Meighen's Government was defeated and the Governor General then granted a dissolution of the House. In the subsequent election the Customs scandal was largely forgotten, and the question of the Governor General's refusal to grant dissolution at King's request became a central issue in the election. King won this election, and many Canadians have concluded that his winning answered the question of what the position of the Governor General is, with respect to a request for dissolution from the Prime Minister. Mr. King, during the election, strongly hinted that there was a taint of colonialism surrounding the actions of the Governor General. It must, however, be remembered that Lord Byng quite rightly refused, at any time, to seek the advice of any British officials and, instead, steadfastly acted solely on his own initiative.

Did the Byng crisis, and the subsequent election of 1926, resolve the question of the Governor General's conventional position with respect to dissolution? It is our view that it did not. The Governor General should be, in certain circumstances, entitled to exercise some freedom of choice with respect to the granting of dissolution. It is one of the central themes of this book that the federal Prime Minister and the provincial Premiers are uniquely powerful, in terms of western democratic constitutional systems. It is therefore surprising to see men of supposedly liberal persuasion arguing that the Byng crisis stripped the last vestige of freedom of choice from the Governor General. In view of the tremendous power possessed by the Prime Minister in the Canadian constitutional system, surely we should attempt to retain some element of countervailing power to protect us from an excessively ruthless and ambitious Prime Minister, or one who seeks an endless number of dissolutions, in order to achieve his political ends. On the other hand, the Governor General should not refuse lightly a request for dissolution by a Prime Minister. He can exercise some freedom of choice only if certain conditions are present. First, the House must be so constituted that an alternative government can be formed. Secondly, an election should have been held only a short time before the request for dissolution is made. This is urged because the chief argument for supporting the Governor General's position in this kind of situation is largely based on the proposition that too frequent elections bring our political system into disrepute. The electorate must be protected from being bullied into giving a majority through frequent resort to elections. Thus, when one takes into account the conditions required before the Governor General can exercise some independence of judgment, one will realize that there is no great harm — and in our view there is considerable merit — in allowing the Governor General, in these special circumstances, to have the conventional right to refuse dissolution.

The major responsibility of the Governor General is to make certain that a government is in office at all times, in order to carry on the governing of the country. Usually the choice is simple, in that the Governor General calls upon the leader of the party with the largest number of seats to form a Government. In the election of 1925, just mentioned, Mr. King did not obtain the largest number of seats, but decided, as was his right, to remain in office and meet the House. In all other situations, however, where the government has resigned, the business of the Governor General is to ask a member of the House to form a government. There have been no occasions in Canada when this has presented any difficulties. There might arise, however, the situation where the leader of the government party, the Prime Minister, dies while in office. It would then fall to the Governor General to select another member of the party in office to form an administration. We have no recent precedents in Canada for how this would be done by a Governor General, though there are a number of precedents from British experience. Some of the provincial precedents for this are treated later when the office of Lieutenant-Governor is discussed.

Before leaving the office of Governor General we must underline again the fact that the conventions surrounding the functioning of this officer have contributed, as have a number of other legal principles and conventional rules, to building up the power and political effectiveness of the Prime Minister. For example, one need only note a minute of the Privy Council, P.C. 3374, issued on October 25, 1935, to realize the full extent of this statement. This minute provides that, "The following recommendations are the special prerogative of the Prime Minister: Dissolution and Convocation of Parliament: Appointment of — Privy Councillors; Cabinet Ministers; Lieutenant-Governors (including leave of absence to same); Provincial Administrators; Speaker of the Senate; Chief Justices of all Courts; Senators; Sub-Committees of Council; Treasury Board;. . . .''[7] These functions are legally vested in the Governor General, but convention has made them political responsibilities of the Prime Minister. If one remembers, from the discussion in the section of this book dealing with delegation, that the majority of delegated powers in this country are assigned to the Cabinet, which is controlled by the Prime Minister, one sees the very powerful position exercised by this person. This is also true if one remembers the doctrine of the supremacy of Parliament, whereby Parliament dominates the courts, and then recalls that Parliament is largely controlled by the Prime Minister. It has always, therefore, been rather surprising to us that persons would complain about leaving the Governor General with even a small measure of independent judgment in connection with dissolution of the House of Commons.

It is ironic that one of our least important offices, in terms of collective political power, has been the subject of one of the most carefully documented studies prepared on any aspect of the Canadian constitution. Professor John Saywell, in his book *The Office of Lieutenant-Governor*, has given us a definitive analysis of that office.[8] It is, accordingly, very difficult, if not impossible, to add anything to his exhaustive study of the subject. At the same time, one cannot completely by-pass the office of Lieutenant-Governor in a work of this kind. There are a substantial number of sections in the British North America Act dealing with the office of Lieutenant-Governor. Section 58 provides that there shall be a Lieutenant-Governor in each province, and also provides for his appointment, by the Governor General-in-Council, by instrument under the Great Seal of Canada. Section 59 provides that he hold office at the pleasure of the Governor General, but shall only be removable, within the first five years of his appointment, for specifically defined cause. It is not uncommon, however, for a Lieutenant-Governor's term to be extended beyond the five-year limit, but usually for one or two extra years at the most.

Section 60 provides that the salary of the Lieutenant-Governor "shall be fixed and provided by the Parliament of Canada." This is an interesting provision, as it substantiates the claim made by Saywell that the original intention was to make the Lieutenant-Governor a federal officer and a spokesman for the federal government within the provincial arena. It was undoubtedly envisaged that the Lieutenant-

Governor would keep the provinces in line and, in particular, would help supervise the protection of minority rights on behalf of the Canadian government.[9] In addition, the British North America Act was drafted in such a manner as to give the Lieutenant-Governor the authority to make certain that provincial legislation does not offend federal authorities. This is amply demonstrated by reference to Section 90. This section gives the Lieutenant-Governor authority to assent to a bill passed by the legislative assembly, to refuse assent, or to reserve the bill for the pleasure of the Governor General. This, in essence, means the pleasure of the federal Cabinet, because of the convention that the Governor General would, in a matter of this kind, act on their advice. This power of reservation was frequently used by Lieutenant-Governors in the period shortly after Confederation. By 1957, when Professor Saywell's book was published, sixty-nine bills had been reserved, of which only thirteen ultimately received the assent of the Governor General. It is interesting to note, however, that forty-two of these reservations had taken place in the first twenty-one years after Confederation, and only twenty-eight had been reserved after 1888. Since 1914, only seven had been reserved, and only one since 1937.[10]

Many provincial politicians have been unhappy about the power of reservation vested in the Lieutenant-Governor, and also about the power vested in the federal government to disallow any acts passed by the provincial legislatures.[11] At one time considerable concern was expressed about the legal validity of the reservation power of the Lieutenant-Governor and the power of disallowance given to the Governor-in-Council. In order to resolve this issue the matter was referred to the Supreme Court of Canada, which unanimously decided that both these powers were still legally valid.[12] It is, however, very clear that, though legally they are still in existence, convention has almost nullified the utilization of these very potent legal weapons possessed by the Lieutenant-Governor and the Governor General respectively. It seems almost inevitable, if the Canadian Constitution should ever undergo widespread revision, that these will be two of the provisions to be either substantially altered or, more likely, totally removed. During the 1971 discussions concerning the Victoria Charter, Prime Minister Trudeau indicated that he was prepared to agree to the removal from the Canadian Constitution of the provisions for reservation and disallowance.

Section 90 of the Act also vests in the Lieutenant-Governor the right to give or refuse assent to bills passed by the Legislative Assembly of the province. It would now be considered almost unthinkable for a Lieutenant-Governor to refuse assent. Historically, however, this has not always been the case, for on twenty-eight occasions provincial Lieutenant-Governors have withheld their assent from bills passed by the legislatures of their respective provinces. Saywell, however, points out that, in twenty-seven of these cases, assent was withheld on the advice, or at least with the approval, of the provincial Cabinet.

There are a number of other sections in the British North America Act, in addition to those already referred to, dealing with the legal power of the Lieutenant-Governor.[13] The chief function of the Lieutenant-Governor, however, within the provincial constitutional structure, is similar to that of the Governor General, namely, making certain that there is always a government in office. Thus, the Lieutenant-Governor is called upon to follow the traditional convention surrounding the selection of a person in the Legislative Assembly to form an administration. As would the monarch or the Governor General, he usually calls upon the leader of the party with the largest number of seats in the legislature to form a government. Traditional British practice has been to allow the monarch, after seeking the advice of relevant persons, to have some degree of freedom of choice, where the issue of who should be Prime Minister is in doubt. This freedom of choice was exercised when Prime Minister Eden resigned after the Suez crisis and the monarch had considerable latitude in deciding who should be called upon to form a government. In this instance, Queen Elizabeth, after consulting several statesmen and other persons within Conservative Party ranks, made her own personal choice.

Professor J. Mallory, in an article in connection with the successions to Premiers Duplessis and Sauvé in Quebec, has cast doubt on whether a provincial Lieutenant-Governor would be allowed this amount of latitude in selecting someone as Premier, in a case in which the succession was uncertain.[14] Professor Mallory points out that, upon the deaths of both Premier Duplessis and Premier Sauvé, similar courses of action were taken by the former members of those Premiers' Cabinets and the party caucuses. The procedure employed consisted of the former Cabinet ministers meeting together, selecting a successor to the dead Premier, and then having their choice endorsed by the party caucus. A petition was then taken to the Lieutenant-Governor who, in each case, called upon the man named by the petitioners. Perhaps the Lieutenant-Governor's constitutional position is now so weak that even the limited right to choose between alternative candidates for the premiership might be denied to him.

Among the other legal rights of the provincial Lieutenant-Governor is that of dismissal. Five provincial governments have been dismissed by Lieutenant-Governors, but the last case occurred in 1903. It is, accordingly, very difficult to imagine this power being exercised by a contemporary Lieutenant-Governor. It is our view, however, that this is a legal power which it is desirable to retain. As has been pointed out on a number of occasions, there are relatively few legal techniques for controlling the federal Prime Minister or the provincial Premiers. The threat of dismissal could, in certain very special circumstances, be a very valuable tool in the hands of a courageous Lieutenant-Governor. On one occasion at least, the threat by a Lieutenant-Governor of utilizing his power of dismissal operated very clearly in the public interest. In 1915, in Manitoba, the Conservative Government of Premier Sir Redmond Roblin was involved in some improper activities in connection with certain government construction contracts. The Government was reluctant to institute an objective and full investigation into the circumstances surrounding this potential scandal. The Lieutenant-

Governor, however, told Premier Roblin that unless a fair and impartial royal commission was appointed he would exercise his prerogative power and dismiss the Government from office. This threat resulted in the appointment of an objective royal commission which uncovered considerable evidence of wrongdoing on the part of the Government. The resignation of the Premier followed and a new Government was formed by the Leader of the Opposition. Though the circumstances in which a Lieutenant-Governor should exercise his right to dismiss a government will rarely occur, there should be retained the constitutional, as distinguished from the legal, right of the Lieutenant-Governor to utilize this weapon in appropriate circumstances, such as the Roblin case.[15]

On three occasions Lieutenant-Governors have exercised their legal right of refusing to grant a dissolution of the legislature. Once again, all of these decisions were taken early in our constitutional history, with the last one occurring in 1891. All of these refusals appear to have been justifiable and were sustained by the legislature and by the electorate at the next test at the polls. Professor Saywell points out that each of these cases concerned a recently elected legislature where the Government no longer had the support of the Legislative Assembly.[16] In addition, an alternative government could be called upon to form an administration without the necessity of a new election. Thus we can see from these three examples that the conditions mentioned in connection with dissolution by the Governor General were satisfied, namely, that there had recently been an election, and that there was an alternative administration prepared to carry on. There is no doubt, though, that in the present contemporary scene it would be very difficult for either the Governor General or a Lieutenant-Governor to refuse dissolution. Once again, however, it is our view that the Governor General and the Lieutenant-Governors should not be totally stripped of this constitutional right.

Before the office of Lieutenant-Governor is left, reference should be made to the leading case dealing with this subject. In *The Liquidators of the Maritime Bank of Canada v. The Receiver General of New Brunswick*,[17] the court was, in effect, asked whether the Lieutenant-Governor of New Brunswick was a representative of the sovereign, thereby entitling the Province of New Brunswick to all the prerogative rights. In this case, the Receiver General, on behalf of the province, had deposited $35,000 in the Maritime Bank of Canada. The bank went out of business and accordingly began to wind up its financial affairs. The main question which had to be resolved by the court was whether the province had priority over other depositors and simple contract creditors of the bank. It would, of course, only have first priority if it could claim the special rights that are part of the royal prerogative. Counsel for the Maritime Bank argued that there was no longer any direct connection between the Crown and the Lieutenant-Governor. In his judgment on behalf of the Judicial Committee of the Privy Council, Lord Watson disagreed with this argument. He reasoned that the appointment of a provincial governor was made by the Governor General-in-Council under the Great Seal of Canada. This meant, he said, that it was an appointment by virtue of the executive government of Canada which, under the terms of Section 9 of the British North America Act, was declared "to continue and be vested in the Queen." He went on to state, "The act of the Governor-General and his Council in making the appointment is, within the meaning of the statute, the act of the Crown, and a Lieutenant-Governor, when appointed, is as much the representative of Her Majesty for all purposes of provincial government as the Governor-General himself is for all purposes of Dominion government." This meant that a provincial government, like the federal government, has first claim to any debts owed to it by any bankrupt organization. This case is significant, not only in terms of the extra-legal rights it vests in the provincial government, but also because of the prestige which it accorded Canadian provincial governments. When combined with the Hodge case, which made the provincial legislatures supreme within their sphere, this decision greatly enhanced the status of the provinces in the political life of Canada. After the Hodge and the Maritime Bank cases it was no longer possible to think of the provinces as not much more than municipal institutions, largely functioning under the over-all supervision of the federal government. The effect of these two decisions was to go far in giving the provincial governments not only extra right but also a more prestigious voice in Canada's federal system.

REFERENCES

1. In the United Kingdom see the Crown Proceedings Act, 1947, 10 and 11 Geo. VI, C.44. In Canada see Crown Liability Act, R.S.C., 1970, C-38. In British Columbia see Crown Proceedings Act S.B.C. 1974, C.24.
2. An excellent analysis of the royal prerogative can be found in an article by D. W. Mundell, "Legal Nature of Federal and Provincial Executive Government: Some Comments on Transactions Between Them," Osgoode Hall Law Journal, vol. 2, no. 1 (April 1960), p. 56.
   Mundell points out that the use of the term "Crown" is very misleading. He stresses that the sovereign is a person for legal purposes, but one who is in possession of a special position by virtue of the prerogative. Those special rights and priveleges accrue to Her Majesty personally but, since she is head of state, they therefore accrue to the government of the day. This recognition of Her Majesty as merely a person with certain extra rights removes much of the mysticism surrounding the term "Crown."
3. All members of the Cabinet are also sworn in as Privy Councillors. The Cabinet is the functioning part of the Privy Council, the entire membership of the latter body having only met on one or two occasions.
4. Judges of the Supreme Court of Canada are appointed by the Governor-in-Council. See Supreme Court Act, R.S.C., 1970, C. S-19, S. 4. Judges of the Federal Court of Canada are also appointed by the Governor-in-Council. See Federal Court Act, R.S.C., 1970 (2nd supp.), C.10, S. 5(2).
5. See E. Forsey, The Royal Power of Dissolution of Parliament in the Commonwealth, Oxford University Press, Toronto, 1943. See in particular pp. 131-40.
   See also R. Graham (ed), The King-Byng Affair 1926: A Question of Responsible Government, Copp Clark, Toronto, 1967.
6. R. Graham, Arthur Meighen, a Biography, Vol. II: And Fortune Fled, 1920-1927, Clarke Irwin, Toronto, 1963, pp. 419-23.

7. This minute can be found in P. Fox, *Politics: Canada*, 2nd ed., McGraw-Hill, Toronto, 1966, p. 213.
8. J. Saywell, *The Office of Lieutenant-Governor*, University of Toronto Press, Toronto, 1957.
9. J. Saywell, *The Office of Lieutenant-Governor*, ch. 7, "A Federal Officer," p. 162.
10. J. Saywell, *The Office of Lieutenant-Governor*, p. 210. Saywell's statistics are now inaccurate by one, because, since his book was published, there has been a reservation by a Lieutenant-Governor of Saskatchewan. The circumstances of this most recent reservation are described by Professor J. Mallory in his article, "The Lieutenant-Governor's Discretionary Powers: The Reservation of Bill 56," *The Canadian Journal of Economics and Political Science*, vol. 27, no. 4 (November 1961), p. 518. As Professor Mallory points out, the federal government was surprised by this unexpected action. It hastily tabled in the House of Commons an order-in-council stating that, "His Excellency the Governor General by and with the advice of Her Majesty the Queen's privy council for Canada declares his assent to Bill No. 56 of the legislature of Saskatchewan passed during the present year and which was reserved by the Lieutenant Governor of Saskatchewan for the signification of the pleasure of the Governor General in accordance with the terms of the British North America Act."
11. Disallowance is the power vested in the Governor-in-Council to veto statutes passed by provincial legislatures. There have been 112 acts disallowed by the central government, though the overwhelming majority of these decisions were made in the first thirty years after Confederation. For a list of disallowed statutes see G. V. La Forest, *Disallowance and Reservation of Provincial Legislation*, Department of Justice, 1955, pp. 83-101. No provincial statutes have been disallowed since 1943.
12. *Reference Disallowance and Reservation* [1938], S.C.R. 71.
13. Ss. 63, 67, 69, 71, 77, 82, 85.
14. J. R. Mallory, "The Royal Prerogative in Canada: The Selection of Successors to Mr. Duplessis and Mr. Sauvé," *Canadian Journal of Economics and Political Science*, vol. 26, no. 2 (May 1960), p. 314.
15. For a complete description of the Roblin incident see J. Saywell, *The Office of Lieutenant-Governor*, pp. 49-52.
16. See J. Saywell, *The Office of Lieutenant-Governor*, p. 152.
17. *The Liquidation of the Maritime Bank of Canada v. the Receiver General of New Brunswick* (1892), A.C. 437.

Five

The Judiciary

The main guidelines with respect to the organization of the judicial system in Canada are provided within the framework of the British North America Act, but the principles determining the role and functioning of the judiciary are rooted in Anglo-Canadian history. Though it is essential to understand the formal structure of the judicial machinery and the techniques for the appointment and removal of judges, it is far more important to understand how the judiciary interacts with other governmental organs. Overriding all other considerations in defining the special position of the judiciary is the concept of judicial independence. Perhaps no concept is more important to the individual as far as his degree of freedom within the community is concerned. It is difficult to envisage constitutionalism, in the sense of some degree of shared power and limitation on power, operating effectively without a recognition of the independence of the judiciary.

Judicial independence means freedom from accountability to other authorities in the constitutional system. Unlike the Cabinet, boards and commissions, and the civil service, the judiciary is not responsible, in the making of any of its decisions, or in the sum total of its decision-making, to Parliament or to any other body, including the electorate. The judges are free to make their decisions without fear of coercion, threat, sanction or reward of any kind. Totalitarian regimes, on the other hand, blatantly use the courts as just another method of enforcing the will of the power-holders.

Judicial independence is promoted within our constitutional system in a variety of ways. First, it is made especially difficult to remove judges as compared with other office-holders. Furthermore, judges' salaries are specified in a separate statute, as being distinct from other parts of the departmental estimates. No minister of the Crown is held accountable in Parliament for the actions of the judiciary. Leaving these special provisions aside, however, the independence of the judiciary, like most of our constitutional traditions, is preserved and promoted largely by a consensus of opinion that the judiciary should remain free from external coercion. Though, as mentioned above, there are a variety of methods utilized to underline judicial independence, none of these would be particularly effective if a government, supported by the majority of the people, wished to destroy judicial independence. Much of our constitutional structure is unfamiliar to the average citizen. Nevertheless, it is our view that there is a very generally shared consensus among the nation's citizens about certain basic and fundamental matters. One of these root values, which is probably as widely held as any within Canada, is the average citizen's confidence that our courts are free from political manipulation, and his belief that they should remain so. Respect for the courts and obedience to the judiciary's decisions must rely, to a considerable extent, on popular confidence. The general public will only have confidence in a judiciary that operates independently of the Cabinet and Parliament of the day.

Though Canada has a federal system, it has a reasonably unified judicial hierarchy. The British North America Act has vested power in both the provincial legislatures and the federal Parliament to create certain courts. Section 92, subsection 14, of the British North America Act provides that the legislature of a province has the responsibility for "the Administration of Justice in the Province, including the Constitution, Maintenance, and Organization of Provincial Courts, both of Civil and of Criminal Jurisdiction and including Procedure in Civil Matters in those Courts." This provision means that the provinces are free to establish whatever courts they think are necessary. It gives them authority to define the jurisdiction of these courts and the number of judges, and it vests in them the power to determine procedure in civil matters, though the federal Parliament is left with the authority to determine procedure in criminal matters. Thus, it is quite conceivable that the judicial hierarchy can vary from one province to another. In practice there is little difference between the organization of the courts in different provinces. The general pattern is to establish three levels of trial courts and one court of appeal for the province. At the bottom of the judicial hierarchy there is usually provision for family and juvenile courts, small debts court and magistrates' courts for criminal matters. Above these courts is usually an intermediate type of trial court invariably called a district or county court.[1] Above the county court one usually finds a highest court of first instance, usually entitled a supreme, superior or high court. As already mentioned, above these levels of trial courts there is usually a provincial court of appeal.

It is also important to note that, not only are the provincial authorities responsible for organizing and establishing these courts and laying down their jurisdictions, but also they have over-all responsibility for the conduct of judicial administration within the province. This means that the provinces are responsible for establishing the physical quarters in which the judiciary must function. In addition, the responsibility for the enforcement of the criminal law is vested in the provincial authorities. Therefore, except in a few cases, such as narcotics and

a few other special areas, where the federal authorities assume responsibility, we find that the responsibility for enforcing the terms of the
Criminal Code rests with the Attorney-General of the province. It is in
him that the major responsibility rests for seeing that the system of
justice works. This does not mean that the judges are in any way accountable to the Attorney-General, but the Attorney-General does have
an overriding responsibility for the administration of justice, and this
includes guiding through the provincial legislature any legislation
dealing with the organization and jurisdiction of the courts. In many
large cities this responsibility for criminal law enforcement rests with
the municipalities, but over-all responsibility rests with the provincial
Attorney-General.

The federal Parliament also has responsibilities with respect to the
creation, organization and maintenance of courts. Section 101 of the
British North America Act provides that, "The Parliament of Canada
may, notwithstanding anything in this Act, from Time to Time provide
for the Constitution, Maintenance, and Organization of a General Court
of Appeal for Canada, and for the Establishment of any additional
Courts for the better Administration of the Laws of Canada." Under the
terms of this section of the British North America Act the federal Parliament has established two courts: the Supreme Court of Canada and the
Federal Court of Canada. The Supreme Court of Canada sits at the top of
each provincial hierarchy and that of the Yukon and Northwest Territories. Under the provisions laid down by statute a litigant can proceed from the highest provincial court and from the Federal Court to
the Supreme Court of Canada. The Supreme Court of Canada is examined later in this chapter, in terms of its historical origin, jurisdiction and role within the Canadian constitutional framework. The Federal Court of Canada is the successor to the Exchequer Court. The Court
is divided into two divisions, namely the Federal Court — Trial Division, and the Federal Court — Appeal Division. The Federal Court assumed all of the jurisdiction previously exercised by the Exchequer
Court and, in addition, was given further responsibilities. Illustrative of
these responsibilities is the Court's exclusive jurisdiction over claims
by and against the Crown in right of Canada, and claims against or
concerning Crown officers or servants. In addition, litigants can seek
relief from decisions handed down by federal boards, commissions and
other tribunals. It also has authority to decide disputes arising out of
industrial property, admiralty, income tax and estate tax appeals, citi-
zenship appeals and aeronautics. Furthermore, a number of statutes
have express provisions providing for an appeal to the Appeal Division
of the Federal Court, for example: the Broadcasting Act, National
Energy Board Act, Canada Shipping Act and the Immigration Appeal
Board Act. It should also be noted that with the approval of the appropriate provincial legislatures, it has jurisdiction in controversies between provinces or between Canada and a province.

It is worth noting that no court is created by the terms of the British
North America Act itself. All Canadian courts are the creatures of either
the provincial legislatures or the Canadian Parliament. This means that

no court in Canada is immune from ordinary legislative change. For example, the provincial legislature, at any time it wishes, can alter the jurisdiction of the provincial courts. Similarly, the federal Parliament has the power to alter the terms under which the Supreme Court of Canada has been established. Thus, at least in theory, the appropriate legislature, be it federal or provincial, can abolish any court which it has established. This is why it was stressed earlier that judicial independence, to a considerable extent in this country, is dependent upon political good will rather than technical constitutional guarantees. Contrast this situation with the situations in Australia and the United States where national constitutional courts are guaranteed by the terms of the fundamental constitutional document. The failure to provide for a supreme court within the terms of the British North America Act is explicable by virtue of an earlier thesis advanced in this work. It is our view that the men who agreed upon the terms of the British North America Act only performed the minimum task necessary to allow the new nation to function. It was, in fact, not necessary to set up a supreme court for the entire country in 1867, because of the existence, in the United Kingdom, of the Judicial Committee of the Privy Council. The Judicial Committee had, for a number of years, operated as a court hearing appeals from the various British North American colonies. Thus, as long as the Judicial Committee continued to hear appeals there was no pressing need to set up a similar body in Canada to duplicate its work.

Though all appeals to the Judicial Committee of the Privy Council were abolished in 1949, no constitutional study of Canada could possibly ignore the overwhelming importance of the decisions which emanated from this body. Even if Canada should ever adopt an entirely new constitution, the effects of its decision-making will be felt forever. At this point it is not appropriate to discuss the effect of the Privy Council's opinions, but the place it held within the judicial hierarchy in Canada should be examined. Legislation in 1833 provided for the establishment of a committee of the monarch's Privy Council which was to be called the Judicial Committee of the Privy Council. The statute provided that appeals made to His Majesty-in-Council from any order of a court or judge would be referred to this judicial committee, which would then make a report or recommendation to His Majesty-in-Council. The decision was to be made effective by virtue of order-in-council of His Majesty-in-Council. Thus, in a technical sense, the Privy Council was not a court, but to all intents and purposes it functioned as a judicial body. It differed from other judicial bodies within the Anglo-Canadian framework in that, since it was merely recommending to His Majesty-in-Council, it had to do so with one voice. It was therefore the practice of the Judicial Committee to render a decision written by only one of its number. This means that we do not know how the vote went in any particular case that was before the Judicial Committee. In our view this made it more difficult for lower courts to circumvent the decisions of this body, because they could not look to dissents as a basis for drawing up new methods of legal approach. In

1844, by statute, the jurisdiction of the Judicial Committee was extended and remained virtually unchanged until the abolition of appeals from Canada in 1949.[3] One of the significant facts of Canadian constitutional history is that it was possible for appeals to go directly from a court of appeal within a province to the Judicial Committee.[4] This means that many of the most important decisions affecting the division of power in Canada, and other constitutional questions, were never heard by the Supreme Court of Canada.

It was not until 1875 that the Supreme Court of Canada was finally created by federal statute.[5] Two attempts were made to establish such a court prior to 1875, but on both occasions the measures for its creation were withdrawn from the House. It is interesting to note that the second bill was withdrawn largely becasue of Quebec's hostility to it and the feeling that the replacement of the Judicial Committee by a Canadian court appointed by the central government might represent a threat to the legislative jurisdiction of that province. In fact, there were even some misgivings in Quebec upon the abolition of appeals to the Privy Council, and the resting of final jurisdiction in constitutional matters with the Supreme Court of Canada. A large number of French-Canadian constitutional observers have remained critical of the present arrangements with respect to the Supreme Court of Canada. The chief thrust of this argument usually centres on the facts that the Court is a creation of the federal Parliament and that its members are appointed by the federal government. It is argued that this arrangement is not conducive to independent decision-making on the division of legislative powers by the Court.[6]

In the most comprehensive document ever produced in Quebec on consitituional matters, namely the Report of the Royal Commission of Enquiry on Constitutional Problems, usually referred to as the Tremblay Report, great concern was expressed about the fact that the existence of the Supreme Court was not provided for and guaranteed by the fundamental constitutional document.[7] This criticism was met and provided for in the abortive Victoria Charter which, if it had been adopted, would have constituted the Supreme Court of Canada as part of its terms. This in effect would have meant that our highest court would have been entrenched in the Constitution, and its existence would have been put beyond the scope of ordinary legislation. The more difficult question to resolve, however, is whether other substantial changes should be made in the format of the Supreme Court of Canada. One frequently hears the argument that at least some members of the Court should be appointed by the provincial governments. Here again, if the Victoria Charter had been adopted, the proposed Constitution would have provided for a guaranteed role in the appointive process of the provincial authorities. Underlying these proposals is the feeling that in the cases which come before the Court, judges are in some way prone to favour the body that appointed them. There is, as yet, no evidence that the Supreme Court of Canada, despite the fact that its members are appointed by the central government, has tended to render decisions favourable to national legislative claims. Certainly no convincing case has yet been made demonstrating that our judges remain in some way beholden and subservient to the government that appointed them. On balance, however, there seems to be little harm, and probably some benefit in allowing the provinces to participate in the appointment of judges to the Supreme Court of Canada.

Another frequent criticism often made by some Quebec lawyers is that the Supreme Court of Canada, which has only three of its members trained in the civil law and six trained in the common law, hears cases from Quebec on matters coming within the terms of the Quebec Civil Code. Quebec lawyers feel that this has promoted an intrusion of common law ideas into the Quebec legal system. One Quebec law professor has suggested that this problem might be resolved by the establishment of separate common law and civil law chambers of the Supreme Court of Canada.[8] Professor Abel of the University of Toronto takes the view that this matter should be resolved by not allowing appeals in matters of provincial private law to go the Supreme Court.[9]

In our view the Supreme Court of Canada has functioned, if not spectacularly, at least effectively and with no hint of bias due to its organization and constitution. Certainly two fundamental changes seem appropriate. First, as already stated, the Court should probably be embodied in the British North America Act. Secondly, it might become necessary to cut down, to some extent, the private law jurisdiction of the Court in order to allow it more time for public law questions.

Before discussing other matters relating to the functioning of the judiciary in Canada, it is now appropriate to examine briefly some of the terms of the Supreme Court Act.[10] The statute provides that the Court shall consist of a Chief Justice and eight other judges.[11] These men must come from the ranks of the judiciary in Canada, or be lawyers with ten years standing at the Bar.[12] Quebec is given special recognition in relation to the Supreme Court in that, "Three at least of the judges shall be appointed from among the judges of the Court of Queen's Bench, or of the Superior Court, or the barristers or advocates of the Province of Quebec."[13] The reason for this special guarantee to Quebec is to make certain that there are available at least three judges trained in the civil law, to hear cases coming from Quebec. The members of the Court are appointed by the Governor-in-Council,[14] which in effect means the Cabinet of the day. The judges of the Supreme Court are given the maximum tenure ever given any members of the judiciary in Canada, namely that they hold office "during good behaviour," and are only removable "by the Governor-General on address of the Senate and House of Commons."[15] Furthermore, a judge ceases to hold office upon reaching the age of seventy-five.[16] It is also important to note that all persons who are barristers in any province may practise before the Supreme Court of Canada.[17]

Put necessarily rather crudely, there are four basic avenues of appeal to the Supreme Court of Canada. In very limited circumstances a matter may come as of right; that is to say, the Court has no discretion but is required by statute to hear the case. Secondly, under the terms of the Supreme Court Act, a matter may be appealed to the Supreme Court of Canada, with leave of the provincial Court of Appeal, if the provincial Court feels that it is a matter which ought to be submitted to the Supreme Court.[18] Thirdly, in matters where there is no right of appeal to the Supreme Court, the Court itself may grant the parties leave to have their case heard before it.[19] Finally, and of special interest, are the provisions spelled out in Section 55, allowing the Governor-in-Council to refer for opinion to the Supreme Court "Important questions of Law or Fact." In addition to matters referred to it for consideration by the federal government, the Court must also, on occasion, hear references directed by a provincial authority to its own Court of Appeal. Where a provincial statute says that an appeal lies from the highest court of appeal in the province in a reference case, then the Supreme Court, by the terms of Section 37 of the Supreme Court Act, must hear such an appeal. As will be pointed out later in this chapter, appeals as of right have, by a recent amendment to the Supreme Court Act, been dramatically limited.

It is quite clear from reading Section 55 that Parliament, when it enacted this section, primarily envisaged that reference cases to the Supreme Court would relate mainly to constitutional matters, in particular to those sections of the constitution dealing with the division of legislative powers. Nevertheless, the Governor-in-Council is not restricted to referring constitutional questions to the Supreme Court, but may refer "any other matter, whether or not in the opinion of the Court *ejusdem generis* with the foregoing enumerations. . . ."[20] This means that, although in the foregoing subsections of Section 55 the legislature has specifically spelled out reference cases on constitutional matters, these specific provisions do not exclude the possibility of a reference in other areas. The reference case has been extremely important in the constitutional history of Canada.[21] One writer states that one-third of the Privy Council decisions on constitutional matters were originally references to the courts by federal and provincial cabinets.[22] This means that if governments want to reduce the role played by the courts they can do so by diminishing or abolishing the utilization of this technique of bringing matters before the judiciary. There appears in recent years to have been a decline in the use of the reference case by governments. This is probably due to a number of factors, including the increasing dissatisfaction of the provinces, especially Quebec, with utilizing the courts as a method for the resolution of federal-provincial disputes. For example, the federal Cabinet referred the question of control of off-shore mineral rights to the Supreme Court of Canada in order to determine who had jurisdiction over this matter. Jean Lesage, when he was Premier of Quebec, hinted that Quebec might not recognize the validity of the judgment rendered by the Court on this question. Mr. Lesage, and his successor, the late Mr. Johnson, were certainly not alone among provincial Premiers in their reservations about using the courts as a vehicle for the resolution of federal-provincial disputes. Late in 1966, British Columbia claimed jurisdiction over the continental shelf, an area extending several hundred miles off the west coast. This can be interpreted as a move to underline the provinces' wish to resolve these matters other than by judicial decision.

It is now necessary to complete the analysis of the terms of the British North America Act dealing with the judiciary. It is interesting to note how few sections of the Act are devoted to the courts. Under heading VII, entitled "The Judicature," there are only six sections, one of which (Section 101) has already been discussed. Section 96 deals with the appointment of judges to superior, district and county courts in the provinces. It is provided in this section that the appointment of judges to these courts shall be made by the Governor General. This in effect means the Governor General acting on the advice of the federal Cabinet. The appointment of judges to the Federal Court of Canada and the Supreme Court of Canada is, of course, not referred to in the British North America Act, as these courts were not in existence at the time the Act was passed. In the statutes creating both the Supreme Court[23] and the Federal Court,[24] provision is made for the appointment of judges to these courts by the Governor-in-Council. Although there is no reference in the British North America Act to the appointment of judges below the county court level, by implication this was to be a matter within the jurisdiction of the provincial governments and, in fact, appointments to these courts are made by the provincial authorities. It is also important to note that the salaries of all judges from the county court level and above are paid by the central government,[25] and that judges from the county court level up are removable only by virtue of federal authority.

The only specific section in the British North America Act dealing with the subject of removal of judges from office is Section 99 (1), which provides that "the judges of the superior courts shall hold office during good behaviour, but shall be removable by the Governor-General on address of the Senate and House of Commons." The same pattern for removal, however, has been adopted by the federal Parliament in the Federal Court Act[26] and the Supreme Court Act.[27] Surprisingly, the procedure for the removal of county court judges is not provided for in the British North America Act, but is a simpler matter than is the removal of superior court, Federal Court and Supreme Court of Canada judges. By virtue of federal statute, a county court judge can be removed for "misbehaviour or . . . incapacity or inability to perform his duties properly by reason of age or infirmity."[28] Furthermore, a county court judge can be removed by order-in-council of the federal Cabinet without resort to the Senate and the House of Commons, as is required in the case of higher court judges.[29] Though it is technically not too difficult to remove a judge, it is, in fact, extremely rare for a judge to be removed from office in Canada. Certainly no judge would be removed by the Senate or the House of Commons or, in the case of a county court judge, by order-in-council, without exhaustive investigation by a committee of the House and/or by some commission of enquiry probably conducted by a judge.[30] Furthermore, the term "good behaviour" is interpreted in such a way as to require extremely bad conduct on the part of a judge — conduct probably amounting to bribery, obvious partiality, conviction of a criminal offence, or something of a similarly serious nature — before removal would be considered. Thus, though the federal government has all the machinery within its control for the removal of all county court judges and above, recourse to these techniques has very infrequently been utilized. This illustrates the view, outlined earlier, that judicial independence is based less on positive law contained in either the British North America Act or other statutes than on the attitude of politicians and other citizens toward judges. It is accepted at all levels of our society that a judge must be free to function without fear of reprisal on account of his decisions, and it should be remembered that the tremendous importance attached to judicial independence is reflected in the statutory law in that judges get the maximum protection from removal afforded anyone. In particular, when one compares the legal position of the civil servant with that of the judge, it becomes clear what extensive legal efforts are made to protect the judge. The civil servant holds office only at pleasure and can legally be dismissed on very short notice. Here again, convention operates to protect the civil servant, but the judge is protected, not only by even stronger traditions, but also by the maximum legal protection accorded any persons within our constitutional process. [31]

Canada has, in effect, thirteen judicial hierarchies and two different systems of law. Each province and territory has its own hierarchy of courts, with the Supreme Court of Canada standing at the top of each of these respective hierarchies. In addition, cases heard by the Federal Court of Canada can be appealed to the Supreme Court. All the provincial courts hear disputes based on both federal and provincial law. Leaving aside those matters that must be heard by the Federal Court, all disputes under federal law are heard in courts constituted by the provincial legislatures. Similarly, the Supreme Court of Canada, by granting leave, can hear appeals from the ten provincial hierarchies on matters of purely provincial law. Because of the doctrine of *stare decisis* the Supreme Court of Canada acts as a vehicle for the promotion of some degree of legal uniformity, even in relation to matters coming solely within the legislative jurisdiction of the provinces. [32] Nevertheless, the unifying force of the Supreme Court must not be overestimated, since only a relatively small proportion of cases are ever appealed to this body. This is particularly true since the most recent amendment of the Supreme Court Act abolished appeals as of right, where the amount of money involved exceeded ten thousand dollars. The effect of this amendment will probably be to reduce the number of private law appeals heard by the Supreme Court of Canada. This means that the Court can still play an important role in the future development of provincial civil law, but the number of such cases handled by the Court will probably be dramatically diminished. Thus, the aforementioned change in the jurisdiction of the Supreme Court will result in an ever increasing proportion of private law cases being finally dealt with by provincial courts of appeal, tending to diminish the unifying force of the Supreme Court of Canada in private law matters. This development will undoubtedly be welcomed in Quebec where there has been, within the legal profession, considerable criticism of utilizing the Supreme Court as a court of final recourse in Quebec civil law matters.

Quebec, unlike the other nine provinces, has a system of private law based on European civil law traditions. The European civil law tradition involves outlining the basic rules relating to private law — e.g., contracts, delicts (torts), successions, property, mandate (agency) — in a written code of rules. The Quebec Civil Code, which is at present being revised, was modelled to a considerable extent on the French Civil Code, which in turn had its roots in the Roman law. Quebec lawyers and judges operate a very interesting legal system. They must not only deal with federal and provincial statutes, but also be aware of the common law rules which originally emanated from Great Britain on matters of public law. Furthermore, when dealing with the Criminal Code, which is a federal statute, Quebec lawyers must be aware of common law defences, as these are still retained by virtue of the terms of Section 7 of the Criminal Code of Canada. In additon, however, the Quebec lawyer and judge must be adept at utilizing the concepts of the civil law, which involves some knowledge of Roman and French private law. They must also be familiar with the basically common law type of procedures which are utilized in criminal law matters. In addition, the Quebec Code of Civil Procedure and the organization of the courts in Quebec tend to follow common law patterns rather than those of Europe. Though a common law lawyer from another province in Canada might have considerable difficulty in dealing with civil law problems covered by the Civil Code, he would probably find the provisions of the Quebec Code of Civil Procedure comparable to those existing in his own jurisdiction. For example, judges of Quebec's Court of Appeal can hand down their own individual judgments though, of course, they may, if they wish, concur with a judgment written by one of their brother judges. The French civil law practice provides that only one judge hands down the decision of the court, thus making the common law tradition of the dissenting judge an impossibility. On the other hand, one at least knows what the reason for judgment in a particular case was, as compared with the common law situation where one might find four or five judges all agreeing on the result but reaching it by different analytical routes.

The great theoretical difference between the civil and common law traditions is the attitude of the judge, when making a decision, towards previous judicial precedent. Fundamental to all the common law tradition is the concept of *stare decisis* which, put very crudely, means that the decisions of certain courts are binding on other courts. In theory this might appear to be a very rigid system permitting, especially in the lower courts, very little leeway in deciding the cases that come before them. In reality, however, it is very seldom that two cases are absolutely identical, so that if a court is unhappy with a previous precedent there is usually considerable room for distinguishing the previous decision, that is to say, finding differences between the case at hand and the previous judicial holding.

In a civil law system the judge is not bound in his interpretation of the code by previous judicial decisions. In practice, however, Quebec judges usually give serious consideration to the case law, or, as it is referred to in Quebec, the jurisprudence, in a matter involving the interpretation of the civil code. Some areas of law in Quebec, such as delict (tort), are covered in the code by a very few general provisions, and a true understanding of the law in these areas is possible only by thorough study of the relevant decisions.[33]

Another difference between the civilian lawyer and his common law counterpart is their attitudes toward the writings of legal scholars. The Quebec lawyer and judge, steeped in the tradition of the civil law, accord considerable recognition to the writings of learned legal theorists. The common law tradition, on the other hand, with its heavy emphasis on previous judicial decisions and the doctrine of precedent, has often tended to ignore the writings of legal scholars, though there is some evidence of a changing attitude on the part of common law judges. This perhaps reflects different cultural patterns within the English-speaking and French-speaking segments of Canada. The English-Canadian lawyer tends to approach legal change in a pragmatic way. He is content with resolving one problem at a time until ultimately a theory emerges. The civilian, perhaps reflecting the traditions of his culture, is inclined to prefer to start from a theoretical framework and then attempt to resolve problems according to this previously worked out theory. This cultural difference is very much reflected in the different attitudes of French- and English-speaking Canadians toward constitutional change. The French-speaking politician or intellectual is much more likely to call for a total sweeping away of the existing structure and its replacement by a new, and as definitive as possible, constitutional document. The English-speaking Canadian politician or intellectual is more likely to take the view that, by resolving problems one at a time, ultimately a satisfactory super-structure will be built. This cultural difference in approaches to problem-solving is one which will probably continue to confound the Canadian nation and to result in continued misunderstanding. The French-speaking Canadian will regard the English-speaking Canadian as overly pragmatic. The English-speaking Canadian will take the view that no code, statute or constitution can ever successfully resolve all problems, and that a too-hasty attempt at an over-all solution may create more problems than it solves. Undoubtedly constitutions, codes or statutes become dated or have large gaps and, accordingly, a high degree of pragmatism seems to be inevitable. In fact, a certain part of every Quebec lawyer's time is spent in attempting to circumvent the more archaic provisions of the Quebec Civil Code in order to meet the problems of contemporary society. On the other hand, there is an increasing tendency to codify portions of the private law in the common law world.

The previously mentioned amendment to the jurisdiction of the Supreme Court should relieve some Quebec law teachers' and lawyers' uneasiness about the role of the Court in relation to private law matters. Though the hopes of many Quebec civilians that no case revolving around the interpretation of the Quebec Civil Code can be heard by the

Supreme Court of Canada are not realized, nevertheless it seems certain that a far smaller proportion of Quebec civil law cases will be heard by the Court. The reason for this point of view is that two-thirds of the Court's judges are untrained in the civil law and, therefore, according to these critics, are unsuited to decide matters arising from the provisions of the Quebec Civil Code. In practice, most cases involving the Civil Code of Quebec that come before the Supreme Court of Canada are heard by a five-man bench composed of three civil law judges and two common law judges. Many Quebec spokesmen feel that this is still unsatisfactory.[34] It is unlikely that the presence of two judges trained in common law substantially alters the results of the decisions handed down, but to many civilians the terminology used in the judgments is just as important as the result itself. However, the phenomenon of common law and civil law judges dealing together with problems from each other's jurisdictions is a very interesting one in terms of the development of a distinctly Canadian jurisprudential tradition.

In an earlier section of this book the relationship between the courts and the legislature was defined. It is, however, appropriate to re-emphasize this relationship, as it is so important to the Canadian constitutional system. As stated by Mr. Justice Lyman Duff in the "Persons" case,[35] " . . . the constitution was, nevertheless, to be 'similar in principle' to that of the United Kingdom; a canon involving the acceptance of the doctrine of parliamentary supremacy in two senses, first that Parliament and the legislatures, unlike the legislatures and Congress in the U.S., were, subject to the limitations necessarily imposed by the division of powers between the local and central authorities, to possess, within their several spheres, full jurisdiction, free from control by the courts; . . . "[36] Mr. Justice Duff is restating the classic proposition that, as long as the legislature is acting within its sphere, its statutory enactments cannot be challenged by the courts. He specifically contrasts this with the United States situation. In particular, the United States Supreme Court, asserting its right to interpret the Constitution, has struck down a wide variety of legislative action. Thus, even if Congress is not encroaching on state jurisdiction, if the courts feel that the rights guaranteed by the Constitution — and in practice this usually means the first ten amendments plus the fourteenth amendment — have been infringed, they can declare the legislation unconstitutional. Since the Constitution, including these amendments, is very vaguely worded, the courts have been given a considerable latitude in striking down legislation. Thus, there is virtually no act of either the United States Congress or state legislatures that cannot be overruled as being unconstitutional by at least some part of the American judiciary.

There has been considerable debate in the United States over whether the courts have utilized their powers of judicial review excessively. When Mr. Justice Frankfurter was sitting as a member of the United States Supreme Court, he generally represented the view that Congress and the state legislatures should be the major decision-makers within the nation, and that the courts should be reluctant to strike down legislation as unconstitutional. At the opposite end of the spectrum Justices Black and Douglas have been typical representatives of the activist wing of the Court who have taken the view that the courts must play an active role in striking down any legislation which appears to transgress, if ever so slightly, the provisions of the Constitution.[37]

The doctrine of supremacy of Parliament, however, has not left the courts completely without ability to thwart legislative and executive decisions of which they disapprove. First, the Canadian courts, by virtue of the fact that legislative power is divided, have the authority to declare that a statute does not come within the sphere of legislative power assigned to the legislature which passed the statute. This has often meant that a court, faced with an enactment which it feels violates basic civil liberties, is able to declare the statute beyond the legislative scope of the province or of the federal Parliament, whichever passed the statute. If, using this technique, the courts strike down a statute of a provincial legislature, they can only hope that the federal Parliament will not take this as an invitation to pass similar legislation. In the Padlock case referred to earlier, Mr. Justice Abbott, in a remark not essential to his decision, expressed the view that there were certain subjects beyond the jurisdiction of either the federal or provincial legislatures. This view, however, is very much at variance with the position traditionally taken by Canadian judges.

The ill-fated Victoria Charter of 1971 proposed the entrenchment in the Canadian Constitution of a statement of rights binding on both the federal Parliament and the provincial legislatures. An enactment of this kind would probably be a significant step towards the introduction of an American style relationship between the courts and the legislatures. It is our view that we should not be too hasty about embracing the American system of judicial review. It is imperative that we retain a high degree of faith in our Parliament and legislatures, and leave with these bodies the main responsibility for developing the major policies of the nation. In the United States, because of the doctrine of the separation of powers and the complex working of the congressional system, it has often been difficult to pass legislation. The result has been — as, for example, in the area of civil rights — that the courts have had to substitute themselves for a Congress which often could not pass legislation because of the opposition of a minority of its members. In Canada the executive usually dominates the legislature and therefore there is less need for the courts to act as a result of the failure of the legislators. Furthermore, Canadian legislators have generally demonstrated that they are prudent and sensible men, and it is only with reluctance that we should replace their judgment with that of the judiciary.

Furthermore, as has been touched upon already, Canadian courts are not impotent in their capacity to deal with legislative action. They have, as has been pointed out, the right to declare *ultra vires* a statute that is beyond the jurisdiction of the legislature which passed it. In addition, the courts have established rules of statutory interpretation which often have the effect of dulling the impact of a statute. For example, there is a presumption against retrospective legislation, as it is generally assumed that this type of legislation is undesirable.[38]

These rules of statutory interpretation and presumptions relating to legislation almost amount to a common law bill of rights. For example, it is presumed that Parliament does not intend to deny a citizen access to the courts. It is presumed that if property is taken away there is a right to compensation. It is a rule of statutory interpretation that tax and criminal statutes are interpreted strictly. It must be remembered, however, that these are principles devised by the courts, which have, at the same time, always held that if the legislature clearly desires to rebut one of these presumptions it is capable of doing so.[39] It is, however, quite possible that if Canada's legislators began an excessive intrusion into human rights Canadian judges would declare their actions unconstitutional. Thus we might see the development of a judicial bill of rights in the sense that certain activities would be declared beyond the capacity of any legislative body. This is certainly an alternative to the entrenchment of a bill of rights in the Constitution. It remains our view, however, that in the overwhelming majority of instances, the destiny of the nation and its major conflicts must be resolved by the elected representatives of the people rather than the judiciary, but that in certain instances some kind of ultimate brake might be necessary.[40]

The courts have been more aggressive in the area of administrative law than they have been in other respects. The term "administrative law" is used here to describe the control the courts exercise over actions of administrative officials. First, the courts will prevent governmental officials from going beyond the ambit allowed to them by law. This is known as the doctrine of *ultra vires*, which simply means that a governmental official or body must act within the limit of the power allowed by statute. In addition, however, the courts have evolved a doctrine that if a governmental body or official is exercising a judicial or quasi-judicial function, he must act in accordance with the principles of natural justice; otherwise the decision will be quashed.[41] There are at least two fundamental and basically agreed-upon principles of natural justice, a violation of which will result in a quashing of an administrative decision by the courts. The first of these principles is that, in a quasi-judicial or a judicial matter, there is a right to a hearing — or, as it is often referred to, *audi alteram partem*: "Hear the other side." The other fundamental principle of natural justice is that no man should be a judge in his own cause. This is often referred to as the rule against bias on the part of the deciding authority. Many authorities would argue that the principles of natural justice are merely a part of the doctrine of *ultra vires* and, in effect, amount to an implication that Parliament intends any authority it delegates to be exercised in accordance with certain basic principles. Looked at from this point of view, the principles of natural justice are similar to the presumptions the courts apply in the task of statutory interpretation. Presumably, if the doctrine of the supremacy of Parliament is fully operative, the legislature is entitled to provide that the principles of natural justice do not apply and that, for example, a man can be deprived of certain rights without a hearing. It is quite likely that the courts could find some method of combating this type of legislative pronouncement, certainly in the area of federal agencies or officials, resort could be had to the Canadian Bill of Rights. This is illustrated by the fact that in any event attempts on the part of the legislatures to prohibit judicial control of administrative action by statutory provision (called privative clauses) have invariably failed.

This analysis of the principles of natural justice raises again the question of the extent to which the judiciary should impose its procedures on other officials within the constitutional process. Many matters were taken away from the courts and given deliberately to administrative tribunals, mainly because of the costliness and time-consuming nature of the judicial process. On the other hand, are there not certain basic procedures which should always be followed, irrespective of the time and cost involved? Canadian courts cannot be accused of excessive interference with the administrative process. The courts only impose a bare minimum of procedural rules on administrators when certain types of responsibilities are being discharged. Even in the instances in which procedures have been imposed, they have been of a very general and broad nature. The courts have certainly not attempted to impose on administrative authorities all the details of the normal judicial hearing. Furthermore, the courts have restricted their control of administrative action to situations where there has been a violation of jurisdiction or a denial of the principles of natural justice. The courts have consistently refused to substitute their view of the merits of a case for that of the deciding officers. This reflects the view that policy is a matter for the legislators and their delegatees.

The chief impact of the judiciary, in particular the Privy Council, on the Canadian constitutional structure has been in the courts' interpretation of those sections of the British North America Act dividing legislative power, especially Sections 91 and 92. Until recently, most of the scholarly writing on the subject of the Canadian Constitution has focused on the judicial decisions relating to these two sections. It is not, therefore, our intention to do a detailed analysis of the very large number of decisions interpreting these because, as has already been pointed out, there have been frequent competent academic contributions on the subject and, in addition, a full treatment of this area would of itself require a separate book.[42] Put as simply as possible, the main result of the judicial interpretations of Sections 91 and 92 has been to render provincial legislative jurisdiction considerably wider than was probably envisaged by the Fathers of Confederation. A reading of Sections 91 and 92 justifies the claim that their original intention was to create a nation with a strong central government and relatively weak provincial authority. Section 91 bestows on the federal Parliament the authority to "make Laws for the Peace, Order and good Government of Canada, in relation to all Matters not coming within the Classes of Subjects by this Act assigned exclusively to the Legislatures of the Provinces; . . ." This is the phrase which vests general legislative powers in the central Parliament, subject to those specifically designated areas assigned to the provincial legislatures. Unlike the United States, where residual power rests with the states, it was clearly the intention in Canada to vest residual authority in the federal Parliament. That is to say, anything not specifically assigned to the provincial legislatures was to reside with the Parliament of Canada. The introductory words of Section 91, however, did not conclude with the above quotation, but rather went on to say, "and for greater Certainty, but not so as to restrict the Generality of the foregoing Terms of this Section, it is hereby declared that (notwithstanding anything in this Act) the exclusive Legislative Authority of the Parliament of Canada extends to all Matters coming within the Classes of Subjects next herein-after enumerated. . . ." The Act then goes on to list a number of examples of the general authority upon which the federal Parliament can legislate under its "Peace, Order and good Government" power. At the end of the examples of federal parliamentary jurisdiction the section provides that any of the stated examples shall be construed as not coming within the class of matters referred to as local or private in Section 92. It is shown later how this latter provision (often referred to as the deeming clause) was used by the judges to isolate the enumerated headings of Section 91 from the general phrase "Peace, Order and good Government," thereby undermining the impact of the clause. In Section 92 the language is straightforward and merely prescribes that "In each Province the Legislature may exclusively make Laws in relation to Matters coming within the Classes of Subjects next herein-after enumerated." The section then lists sixteen classes of subjects upon which the provincial legislature is entitled to enact legislation.

The chief impact of the courts, including the Privy Council, has been to distort seriously the intentions of the Fathers of Confederation, by their interpretation of Sections 91 and 92. For the moment let us ignore whether the result of these decisions has been desirable or undesirable, and concentrate on the actual decision-making of the courts. First, it must be emphasized that the majority of key decisions interpreting Sections 91 and 92 were made by the Judicial Committee of the Privy Council. True, there have been a few decisions on the division of legislative power since 1949, but by and large the major disputes concerning legislative jurisdiction had been determined prior to 1949, by cases brought before the Privy Council. Furthermore, a substantial proportion of the most important Privy Council decisions were written by two men, Lord Watson and Lord Haldane. Both of these men showed a strong predilection for striking down federal legislation or, conversely, upholding the validity of provincial legislation. A great deal of speculation has been undertaken on why these particular men so favoured provincial legislative claims, but as yet no definite answer has appeared. Certainly, the fact that Lord Haldane was retained as counsel for the provinces in a number of cases which appeared before the Privy Council, and in particular before Lord Watson, must have been a factor in influencing his judgment.[43] It has also been suggested that Haldane, being a nineteenth-century liberal, would have been opposed to centralist power as a potential threat to the unhampered operation of *laissez faire* capitalism.[44] Professor Lower has suggested that Watson and Haldane objected to a strong central government in Canada because it represented a threat to imperial unity.[45] Furthermore, it is quite possible that both Watson and Haldane were genuinely alarmed lest the central government threaten the rather feeble autonomy of the provinces generally and, in particular, Quebec. Perhaps these men saw the provinces as underdogs in their struggle with the federal government, and they wished to even up the struggle somewhat by holding federal legislative claims to a minimum. There is no doubt that Quebec owes both Haldane and Watson considerable gratitude for the decisions they made with respect to the division of legislative power. It is therefore not hard to understand why many Quebec spokesmen were concerned about the abolition of appeals to the Privy Council, even though at the same time it galled them that they were to a considerable extent protected by British judges.

Another criticism one frequently hears of the Privy Council's decisions is that they were essentially literal, technical interpretations of the British North America Act, rather than broad policy-minded constructions of the words of the Act.[46] It is our view that a narrow, technical construction, or literal reading, of the words of the British North America Act would have led to a series of decisions on Sections 91 and 92 clearly favouring federal jurisdiction, and that the Privy Council took a non-literal approach and replaced application of the actual words of the statute with a clear pursuit of a policy, namely, maximum protection of the provincial legislative position. Many critics of the Privy Council refuse to call this a policy approach simply because they do not like the policy. In other words, any decision that they do not like they label the result of a literal, narrow and technical approach. The favouring of provincial legislative claims is just as much a policy as a widespread favouring of federal legislative jurisdiction.[47]

The great unanswered question of Canadian constitutional law is, what would have been the interpretations of Sections 91 and 92 if recourse to the Privy Council had not been available? In other words, would final decision-making by the Supreme Court of Canada have resulted in an interpretation of Sections 91 and 92 more favourable to federal claims? An over-all examination of the decisions of the Supreme Court of Canada on the division of legislative powers shows that the Court has tended to reflect the position taken by the Privy Council. It is possible, however, that the Supreme Court of Canada felt that it was bound by the decisions of, and the approach to Sections 91 and 92 developed by, the Privy Council. This argument is not completely convincing, because a court can almost always circumvent a decision of a higher court with which it disagrees. There is very little to suggest, prior to 1949 at least, that the Supreme Court of Canada was making any concerted effort to follow a different path from that of the Privy Council. Probably the most famous of Canadian judges, Lyman Duff, tended to hand down rulings favourable to provincial legislative claims. In fairness, however, it must be kept in mind that the Supreme Court of Canada did not have an opportunity to hand down decisions in a substantial proportion of the most important cases on the division of legislative power. One study shows that, of the Privy Council decisions on the Canadian Constitution, 77 out of 159 cases that came before the Privy Council by-passed the Supreme Court of Canada.[48] Furthermore, this study shows that, if analysis is confined to cases that deal with the division of legislative powers in the British North America Act, 73 of 143 cases heard by the Privy Council were appealed directly to it from provincial courts. This means that over half of the cases on the division of legislative powers were never before the Supreme Court of Canada at all. Thus, the Supreme Court's capacity for influencing the trend of decision-making with respect to legislative authority was considerably weakened by the capacity of parties to bypass it as an arbiter.

In the years immediately following its formation, the Supreme Court tended to favour federal legislative claims.[49] Nevertheless, this does not prove that it would have maintained this course if no appeal to the Privy Council had been available. Instead, perhaps both the judges of the Privy Council and the Supreme Court of Canada recognized that the strong centralist type of nation envisaged by Sir John A. Macdonald and his political colleagues was possibly not feasible for a large, under-populated, economically and culturally diverse country such as Canada. Furthermore, a province such as Ontario exercised authority over too large a proportion of the nation's land, wealth and population to remain a glorified municipal government. When these factors are combined with the fact that a third or more of the nation's population has always been French-speaking, with a strong pride in local institutions, perhaps the Privy Council's decisions were wiser than many of its critics would care to admit. It is quite possible that its decision-making was more in accord with the realities and needs of the Canadian political situation than were those of its critics, who continually advocated strong central power. The real question, however, is, "Did the Privy Council go too far in its recognition of provincial legislative claims as against those of the central Parliament?" It is our view that if the Privy Council had slightly modified its provincial rights zeal, it would have struck a very happy balance in terms of the realities and needs of the Canadian polity.

Before the trend of judicial interpretation of Sections 91 and 92 of the British North America Act is examined, it is important to remember two vital decisions relating to the position of the provincial legislatures and executives. It will be recalled, from preceding sections of this work, that, very shortly after Confederation, the Privy Council, in Hodge v. The Queen,[50] held that, within its sphere, the provincial legislature was as sovereign as the Imperial Parliament was in relation to United Kingdom affairs. Then, in the Maritime Bank case, the Privy Council held that the Lieutenant-Governor was the representative of the monarch and, accordingly, exercised all the prerogative powers of the sovereign. These two cases combined to alter the status and legal position of the provinces from that envisaged by the Fathers of Confederation. All that was left for the Privy Council to do in order to boost the provincial position further was to enlarge its area of jurisdiction. In a series of decisions handed down by the Judicial Committee it proceeded to do just that. In effect, it rendered the "Peace, Order and good

Government" phrase in Section 91 a separate ground for legislative authority, independent of the enumerated heads which follow in that section, rather than the basic source of federal power. Watson and Haldane evolved the doctrine that the "Peace, Order and good Government" clause gave the federal Parliament authority only in times of emergency. There were deviations from this position by the Privy Council, as, for example, Viscount Simon's reasoning and decision in the Canada Temperance case.[51] However, to all intents and purposes the emergency doctrine was the predominant one followed during the period of appeals to the Privy Council. Subsequent to the abolition of appeals to that body, the Supreme Court of Canada, in the *Johannesson v. West St. Paul* case,[52] indicated its willingness to see "Peace, Order and good Government" serve as a basis for federal legislative claims in times other than an emergency. This trend has been continued by the Supreme Court in two more recent cases, namely Reference re Offshore Mineral Rights[53] and *Munro v. National Capital Commission*.[54] In both of these cases the federal claims to offshore mineral rights and zoning in the national capital region respectively were sustained by the Court as being valid exercises of the federal Parliament's jurisdiction over peace, order and good government.

The Privy Council thus, leaving aside emergency, boiled its interpretation of Sections 91 and 92 down to a comparison of the enumerated heads in those two sections. Their approach was to examine, first, whether the legislation under consideration came within the enumerated heads of Section 92. If it did not, then presumably it was within federal legislative authority. If, however, it did come within the heads of Section 92, then the Court looked to see whether it was also covered by the enumerated heads of Section 91. In the event that it was a subject covered by heads in both Sections 91 and 92, then federal legislative competence would be established. In practice, however, this often came down to a struggle between the terms of Section 91 (2), "The Regulation of Trade and Commerce" and those of heads 92 (13), "Property and Civil Rights in the Province," and 92 (16), "Generally all Matters of a merely local or private Nature in the province." Here again, in their interpretation of these rather vague heads of power, the Privy Council usually found the legislation to be within the enumerated heads 92 (13) and (16). The federal authority over "The Regulation of Trade and Commerce" proved to be very disappointing as a source of federal authority, except where the matter under consideration was very clearly inter-provincial. The Privy Council blocked attempts to utilize this head of power when the federal Parliament attempted to regulate any businesses operating solely within one province. The usual technique for emasculating Section 91 (2) was to refer to other enumerative heads of Section 91, such as 91 (14) "Currency and Coinage," 91 (15) "Banking," 91 (17) "Weights and Measures," and 91 (18) "Bills of Exchange and Promissory Notes," and argue that if "Trade and Commerce" was meant to be a general over-all power, the British Parliament would not have found it necessary to spell out these particular headings dealing with commercial matters. In other words, the attempt of the Fathers of Confederation to make themselves over-whelmingly clear by postulating examples of "Peace, Order and good Government" and of "Trade and Commerce," had the effect of restricting the general powers conferred rather than reinforcing them by way of concrete examples. The tendency of the Privy Council was to consider the specific examples as being the grant of legislative power rather than the general headings which the examples were supposed to emphasize and illustrate. Thus, Sections 92 (13) and (16) became the catch-all subsections of Sections 91 and 92, for purposes of allocating subject matter which did not very clearly fall within one of the enumerated heads. As a result of this provincially-leaning interpretation of the British North America Act, the federal gains through judicial interpretation have been relatively few, though aeronautics and radio broadcasting were two notable exceptions to this trend.

When one looks, very quickly, at some of the major fields coming within provincial jurisdiction, such as education, roads, natural resources, municipal institutions, a substantial area of social welfare, and labour relations, it is not surprising that the provinces are pressing very strongly for an increased share of the nation's tax resources. Matters such as education, which appeared at the time of Confederation as relatively inexpensive, now involve the expenditure of vast sums. Thus, as a result of several causes, the scheme of Confederation has been thrown out of kilter. The Fathers of Confederation envisaged that the major fields would rest with the federal Parliament and accordingly gave Parliament the power of raising money "by any Mode or System of Taxation" (Section 91 (3)). The provincial legislatures, however, were restricted to "Direct Taxation within the Province in order to the raising of a Revenue for Provincial Purposes." One of the most obvious of Canada's contemporary problems is readjusting the constitutional system so as to provide the provinces with the fiscal means to discharge their legal responsibilities. On the other hand, redistribution of finances must not extend so far as to jeopardize the central government's role within Confederation.

REFERENCES

1. The Province of Quebec is an exception to this practice.
2. See *The Constitution of the United States*, Article 3, Sections 1 and 2, and *Commonwealth of Australia Constitution Act*, 1900 (Imp.), C.12, Sections 71 and 73.
3. A brief history of the Judicial Committee can be found in *British Coal Corporation v. The King* [1935] A.C. at pp. 510-12.
4. See P. Russell, *Leading Constitutional Decisions*, rev. ed., McClelland and Stewart Limited, Toronto, 1973, p. xiii. He states that 77 of 159 constitutional cases decided by the Privy Council came directly from the provincial appeal courts.
5. The developments preceding and following the establishment of the Supreme Court are interestingly detailed by F. MacKinnon, "The Establishment of the Supreme Court of Canada," The Canadian Historical Review, vol. 27, no. 3 (September 1946), p. 258.
6. One of the leading proponents of this point of view is Professor J. Y. Morin, who outlined his position in an article entitled "A Constitutional Court for Canada," *Canadian Bar Review*, vol. 43, no. 4 (December 1965), p. 553. He suggests the estab-

lishment of a separate constitutional court in Canada similar to the one in West Germany. He proposes that this new constitutional tribunal should have an equal number of judges from English- and French-speaking Canada. Under this scheme the judges would be chosen by a newly constituted Senate, which would also have equal representation from English- and French-speaking Canada. Mr. Cheffins has already challenged Professor Morin's proposals, and it is therefore unnecessary to restate his position here. See R. Cheffins, "The Supreme Court of Canada: The Quiet Court in an Unquiet Country," *Osgoode Hall Law Journal*, vol. 4, no. 2 (September 1966), p. 259. For another study of Supreme Court reform see P. Russell, "The Jurisdiction of the Supreme Court of Canada: Present Policies and a Programme for Reform," *Osgoode Hall Law Journal*, vol. 6, no. 1 (October 1968). p. 1.

7. *Report of the Royal Commission of Inquiry on Constitutional Problems, vol. II, Province of Quebec*, 1956, pp. 107-11.
8. This proposal was made by Professor P. A. Crépeau at the Conference on Federalism and the Supreme Court, held in Toronto in November 1964.
9. A. Abel, "The Role of the Supreme Court in Private Law Cases," *Alberta Law Review*, vol. 4, 1965, p. 39. Professor Abel argues, essentially, that Canada should have a dual hierarchy of courts similar to that existing in the United States. Our reasons for opposing this proposal are contained in Mr. Cheffins' article on the Supreme Court of Canada, cited in f.n. 6 above.
10. *R.S.C., 1970*, C.S-19.
11. *R.S.C., 1970*, C.S-19, S. 4.
12. *R.S.C., 1970*, C.S-19, S. 5.
13. *R.S.C., 1970*, C.S-19, S. 6.
14. *R.S.C., 1970*, C.S-19, S. 4.
15. *R.S.C., 1970*, C.S-19, S. 9(1).
16. *R.S.C., 1970*, C.S-19, S. 9(2).
17. *R.S.C., 1970*, C.S-19, S. 22.
18. *R.S.C., 1970*, C.S-19, S. 38.
19. *R.S.C., 1970*, C.S-19, S. 41(1).
20. *R.S.C., 1970*, C.S-19, S. 55(1)(e).
21. G. Rubin, "The Nature, Use and Effect of Reference Cases in Canadian Constitutional Law," *The McGill Law Journal*, vol. 6, no. 3 (March 1960), p. 168.
22. P. Russell, *Leading Constitutional Decisions*, rev. ed., McClelland and Stewart Limited, Toronto, 1973, p. xxiv.
23. *R.S.C., 1970*, C.S-19, S. 4.
24. *R.S.C., 1970*, 2nd supp., C.10, S. 5(2).
25. *B.N.A. Act*, 1867, S. 100.
26. *R.S.C., 1970*, 2nd supp., C.10, S. 8(1).
27. *R.S.C., 1970*, C.S-19, S. 9(1).
28. *R.S.C., 1970*, C.J-1, S. 31.
29. R.M. Dawson, *The Government of Canada*, 5th ed., University of Toronto Press, Toronto, 1970, p. 402.
30. A detailed outline of the removal powers can be found in R. M. Dawson, *The Government of Canada*, 5th ed., University of Toronto Press, Toronto, 1970, pp. 400-2.
31. It should be noted that judges of the Federal Court of Canada must retire at age 70, see *Federal Court Act*, S. 8(2), while other federally appointed judges must retire at age 75, see *B.N.A. Act 1867*, S. 99(2) and *Supreme Court Act*, S. 9(2).
32. A thorough analysis of the doctrine of *stare decisis* and its impact on the role of the Supreme Court of Canada can be found in M. R. MacGuigan, "Precedent and Policy in the Supreme Court," *Canadian Bar Review*, vol. 45, no. 4 (December 1967), p. 627. An interesting study of the Supreme Court of Canada, using the techniques of judicial behaviourism, has been made by S. R. Peck, "The Supreme Court of Canada, 1958-1966: A Search for Policy through Scalogram Analysis," *Canadian Bar Review*, vol. 45, no. 4 (December 1967), p. 666.
33. W. Friedmann, "Stare Decisis at Common Law and Under the Civil Code of Quebec," *Canadian Bar Review*, vol. 31, no. 7 (August-September 1953), p. 723.
34. Most of the apprehensions of many Quebec legal thinkers regarding the Supreme Court and the Canadian legal system are outlined in the Report of the Tremblay

Commission. *Report of the Royal Commission of Inquiry on Constitutional Problems*, vol. III, bk. 1, pp. 288-96. It should be noted that the Commission recommends that Canada have a constitutional court (p. 295), and that all Quebec civil law cases should be finally determined within the Quebec judicial hierarchy (p. 294).

35. *In the matter of a Reference as to the Meaning of the Word "Persons" in Section 24 of the British North America Act, 1867* [1928] S.C.R. 276.
36. [1928] S.C.R. 276 at p. 291.
37. E. McWhinney, *Judicial Review*, University of Toronto Press, Toronto, 1969. See ch. 4, p. 64, and ch. 9, pp. 177-8.
38. In re Immigration Act [1911] 1 W.W.R. 114.
39. See, for example, *Smith v. Callender* [1901] A.C. 297 at p. 305, where Ashbourne, J., states, "It is obviously competent for the legislature, in its wisdom, to make the provisions of an Act of Parliament retrospective."
40. Douglas A. Schmeiser, "The Case Against Entrenchment of a Canadian Bill of Rights," *Dalhousie Law Journal*, vol. 1, no. 1. (September 1973), p. 15.
41. For an excellent and concise exposition on the concept of natural justice see H.W.R. Wade, *Administrative Law*, Oxford University Press, London, 1971, pp. 171-218.
42. There has been a great deal written on this subject. A brief sample of the material available includes *Report to the Honourable the Speaker of the Senate by the Parliamentary Counsel* [William F. O'Connor] *Relating to the Enactment of the British North America Act, 1867, any lack of consonance between its terms and judicial construction of them and cognate matters*, Queen's Printer, Ottawa, 1939, reprinted 1961. This document is usually referred to as "The O'Connor Report."
   See also F. P. Varcoe, *The Constitution of Canada*, The Carswell Company, Toronto, 1965. This book is mainly devoted to an analysis of the cases dealing with the division of legislative power.
   The constitutional law casebook used in Canadian law schools is B. Laskin, *Canadian Constitutional Law*, 4th ed., The Carswell Company, Toronto, 1974. It includes nearly all the cases dealing with the division of legislative powers in Canada, and has valuable commentary on these cases by the author.
   A much briefer casebook has been prepared by P. Russell, *Leading Constitutional Decisions*, rev. ed. McClelland and Stewart, Toronto, 1973. This book also includes a valuable introduction describing judicial interpretation of the B.N.A. Act.
   All the decisions of the Privy Council relating to the B.N.A. Act have been compiled by P. A. Olmstead in *Decisions of the Judicial Committee of the Privy Council relating to The British North America Act, 1867, and the Canadian Constitution 1867-1954*, 3 vols., Queen's Printer, Ottawa, 1954.
   G. P. Browne, *The Judicial Committee of the Privy Council and the British North America Act: An Analysis of the Interpretative Scheme for the Distribution of Legislative Powers*, University of Toronto Press, Toronto, 1967. B. L. Strayer, *Judicial Review of Legislation in Canada*, University of Toronto Press, Toronto, 1968.
43. A. R. Lower, "Theories of Canadian Federalism — Yesterday and Today," in A. R. Lower, F. R. Scott, et al., *Evolving Canadian Federalism*, Duke University Press, Durham, N.C., 1958, p. 36.
44. A. R. Lower, "Theories of Canadian Federalism — Yesterday and Today," in *Evolving Canadian Federalism*, p. 37.
45. A. R. Lower, "Theories of Canadian Federalism — Yesterday and Today," in *Evolving Canadian Federalism*, p. 38.
46. This criticism of the Privy Council's approach is discussed by P. Russell, "The Supreme Court's Interpretation of the Constitution since 1949" in P. Fox, *Politics: Canada*, 3rd ed., McGraw-Hill Company of Canada Limited, Toronto, 1970, pp. 439-52.
47. It is interesting, and perhaps significant, that when the Labour Party was in power in Great Britain, and nominated who was to sit on the Judicial Committee, some of the decisions most favourable to the federal government were made. E.g., *In re Regulation and Control of Aeronautics in Canada* [1932] A.C. 54, *In re Regulation and Control of Radio Communication in Canada* [1932] A.C. 304, *Attorney General for Ontario v. Canada Temperance Federation* [1946] A.C. 193.

48. P. Russell, *Leading Constitutional Decisions*, rev. ed., McClelland and Stewart, Toronto, 1973, p. xiii.
49. For example, see the decision in *Severn v. The Queen* (1878) 2 S.C.R. C.70.
50. *Hodge v. The Queen* (1883) 9 A.C. 117.
51. *Attorney General for Ontario v. Canada Temperance Federation*, [1946] A.C. 193.
52. [1952] 1 S.C.R. 292.
53. [1968] 65 D.L.R. (2nd.) 353.
54. [1966] S.C.R. 663.

Six

The Federal-Provincial
Consultative Process

Perhaps the most interesting development within the Canadian constitutional process has been the ever-increasing use of various types of
federal-provincial meetings. At least for the time being, it appears that
the courts are no longer the focal point for the resolution of disputes
over the allocation of power between the federal and provincial levels
of government. The struggle between the central and regional governments for power has shifted from the courts to a variety of federal-
provincial conferences and committees. The most important of these
meetings are, of course, those between the Prime Minister of Canada
and the Premiers of the ten provinces. It is at conferences attended by
these men, and other key ministerial personnel, that the major tax-
sharing decisions are currently being arrived at. Since control of finances is the basic ingredient of power, it is obvious that any meetings
which resolve the allocation of fiscal resources must be considered
basic to any realistic appraisal of our constitutional and governmental
system. Purists might argue that the decisions reached at federal-
provincial Premiers' conferences are not legally binding and that it is
therefore improper to consider these meetings as part of the process of
authoritative decision-making. Perhaps in a certain narrow sense this
argument is valid, in that agreements reached by the provincial Premiers and federal Prime Minister must be implemented by resort to the
parliamentary process, yet, nevertheless, it would be naive not to recognize that, even though these conferences do not carry with them the
traditional stamp of legality, the decisions reached are seldom challenged by the legislatures involved. Thus, in terms of the effective
reality of the Canadian power process, agreements arrived at through
these conferences are almost certainly assured of legislative acceptance
because of the domination of Canadian legislatures by the executive for
the reasons described earlier.

In the first edition of this book it was necessary to state that the subject of the federal-provincial consultative process had received little systematic attention by writers on Canadian government. Happily this is now no longer true, as there have been several recent works covering this area. In particular, we are indebted to Professor D. V. Smiley for his book *Canada in Question: Federalism in the Seventies*,[1] especially Chapter 3 which deals with the subject of executive federalism, and to Professor Richard Simeon for his book *Federal-Provincial Diplomacy: The making of recent policy in Canada*.[2] These and other books now give us an excellent over-view of the federal-provincial negotiating structure.[3] The founders of Canada were not unaware that some machinery had to exist to enable Canadian federalism to work effectively and, in fact, they did partially foresee this problem when they created the office of Lieutenant-Governor. The Lieutenant-Governor was originally envisaged as being a federal officer entrusted with the responsibility of communicating the view of the national government to provincial authorities and, if necessary, making certain that provincial governments did not step too far off the path deemed correct for them by the National government. Thus, the Lieutenant-Governor was to be the chief formal machine whereby communications would be maintained between the two areas of Canadian governmental power. It is also probable that the political parties were recognized as being an important informal vehicle whereby federal-provincial matters would be resolved behind the scenes. It seems fairly certain that the Fathers of Confederation did not realize that the provinces would grow so powerful or that federal-provincial problems would become so complex. A combination of the Lieutenant-Governor and the informal processes of party politics and the judicial machinery was undoubtedly assumed to be sufficient for the conduct of federal-provincial relations.

Even now the processes of federal-provincial relations are still relatively under-developed when compared with the importance of the problems to be resolved. It is difficult for the external observer, who is not working within the framework of federal-provincial governmental problems, to gain an accurate picture of all the existing techniques whereby federal-provincial negotiations are carried on. This difficulty is increased by the fact that most of these federal-provincial conferences, whether they be at the Prime Minister and Premiers level, or of a more junior type, are closed to the public. One must often rely largely on releases handed to the press by the participants. Further, most of the consultation below the Cabinet level is not reported in the press.

Though now somewhat dated, the most useful detailed description of the machinery utilized to resolve federal-provincial problems is contained in an article published in the journal of the Institute of Public Administration of Canada.[4] E. Gallant points out that the calendar of federal-provincial conferences and meetings for 1965, distributed at the July 1965 Federal-Provincial Conference of Prime Ministers and Premiers, numbered 125 items: a doubling in the number of conferences and committees meeting in a period of only eight years.[5] Mr. Gallant divides these conferences and committees into seven broad groups. The first is federal-provincial committees, and he notes that there were approximately a hundred, including sub-committees, falling within this category. For example, this includes conferences of the Prime Minister and Premiers, gatherings of federal and provincial Ministers of Welfare, a continuing committee on economic and fiscal matters, etc. He also points out that about thirty of these hundred meetings were regional in character, in that not all provinces were represented at them. He gives as an example The Atlantic Fisheries Committee.

Another category of meetings listed by Mr. Gallant is federal advisory councils. These are councils appointed to act as advisory bodies to the federal Cabinet or federal ministers, but provision is made for representation from provincial governments. The procedure is for the council to deliberate on a matter, and once it has reached agreement and the federal minister accepts the advice of the council and receives the approval of the federal Cabinet, then the federal government can make proposals to the provinces with a strong expectation that the provinces will agree. Mr. Gallant gives as examples of this type of organization The Dominion Council of Health, The National Advisory Council on Rehabilitation of Disabled Persons, The Technical and Vocational Training Council, and The National Council of Welfare. As he points out, these councils also have a wide representation from nongovernmental organizations.

Thirdly, he describes the quasi-independent association, which is his name for bodies composed wholly, or almost wholly, of federal and provincial civil servants. In this instance the ministers or civil servants are not bound by governmental instructions, nor, in turn, do their deliberations bind governments; their purpose is to aid in the communication of ideas among people in a particular field of specialization. Examples of this approach are The Canadian Council of Resource Ministers, and The Canadian Association of Administrators of Labour Legislation.

Another category of conference is the interprovincial conference, which functions without federal participation. Quite often these conferences convene in order to evolve a joint approach to the federal government on some matter of importance to all the provinces. They act almost like a provincial caucus in that their purpose is to resolve differences among the provinces, and to provide a common front for them in a later meeting with the federal government. Examples of interprovincial conferences offered by Mr. Gallant are The Mines Conference of Provincial Ministers, and, perhaps the most significant of all, The Conference of Provincial Premiers. These interprovincial gatherings, a relatively new phenomenon compared to the more traditional federal-provincial meetings, are a significant sign of an awakening awareness of common problems on the part of provincial decision-makers.[6]

There have also evolved a number of sub-committees, whose function is to report to some larger federal-provincial body. For example, The Dominion Council of Health has a number of committees reporting to it on a variety of matters. Finally, there are provincial advisory committees designed to advise the provincial governments on specific matters, and these committees often include federal representatives, whose duty is to inform provincial governments of a federal point of view. An example of this type of committee is The Coordinating Committee on Indian Affairs.

Excluding non-governmental associations, Mr. Gallant found that in 1965 there were two conference and committee meetings of the Prime Minister and Premiers, thirteen of ministers, fourteen of deputy ministers, twenty-seven of directors and sixty-five of professional and technical governmental personnel.[7] Included in this grouping, however, are interprovincial meetings between provincial ministers and other provincial officials. As regards subject matter, the largest number of meetings dealt with two areas: health and welfare, with twenty-one meetings, and agriculture, with sixteen.[8] This, of course, is explainable by the fact that these are two areas in which there is overlapping legislative jurisdiction.

The whole field of federal-provincial relations raises questions of what changes should be made in existing arrangements, and, in particular, what extra formalization should be aimed at in the area of federal-provincial functioning. R. M. Burns suggests that a yearly meeting between the Prime Minister and provincial Premiers might be developed as a matter of practice. Furthermore, he urges that there be regular meetings of federal and provincial ministers working in similar fields, such as agriculture, welfare, health, finance and resource development, in order to work out some kind of common national guidelines.[9] The meetings of Ministers of Finance and provincial treasurers is certainly an example of this type of organization. Mr. Burns, however, rejects any suggestion that a permanent secretariat be developed as an underpinning for the machinery of federal-provincial relations.[10] His opposition to this idea is based on the supposition that the notion of a third level of government would be politically unacceptable. Though it perhaps might be in many respects politically unacceptable, it certainly would be a formal recognition of reality. Since some of the most vital decisions with respect to the future of the country are being resolved through the apparatus of federal-provincial meetings, surely a permanent secretariat might contribute to a more effective resolution of problems through the supply of greater information both to the decision-makers and to the general public.

Probably the most important matter to be regularly discussed in federal-provincial conferences is the division of tax resources between the federal and provincial governments.[11] Any student of the British constitution will know that the chief struggle for power in Britain revolved around the raising and the expenditure of public funds. The power of the monarch was ultimately thwarted by Parliament's ability to control taxation. Similarly, one of the main political struggles in Canada is that being waged between the central and regional governments over the division of tax resources. It is necessary to re-examine the original intentions of the founders of the Canadian federal system, so that the existing debate surrounding the division of fiscal resources may be fully understood. As has already been outlined, the Fathers of

Confederation envisaged a strong central government, which was to have jurisdiction over most of the important legislative matters. It therefore followed logically that, in order to exercise its heavy legislative responsibility, the central government should be given maximum capacity for the raising of public funds. Section 91 (3) of the British North America Act provides that the federal Parliament has authority for the "raising of Money by any Mode or System of Taxation." In contrast with this wide taxing power of the federal Parliament is the restricted authority vested in the provincial legislatures by Section 92(2), which reads, "Direct Taxation within the Province in order to the raising of a Revenue for Provincial Purposes." Thus, it should be noted that not only were the provincial governments restricted to direct taxation, but even this power was qualified by the latter part of Section 92(2).

To help the original provinces which entered into Confederation, the British North America Act provided for a series of fiscal arrangements whereby the federal government would compensate the provincial governments by the payment of per-capita grants, and by a wide variety of other special grants to aid the provinces that had special financial problems.[12] Thus, since Canada's formation in 1867, the provinces have never been totally independent of financial help from the central government. There are still a wide variety of special provisions designed to assist the poorer provinces, so that they may provide for their people a standard of living comparable to that in the richer provinces. This concept of sharing the wealth by taking from the richer provinces and distributing among the poor found its most logical and aggressive expression in the report of the Rowell-Sirois Commission, officially known as The Royal Commission on Dominion-Provincial Relations. It sought to achieve this end by having the central government do the taxing and then redistribute money to the provinces so that each would have a relatively equal welfare and educational system for its people. The report, presented in May 1940, was never completely implemented, though the concept of the tax rental agreement by which this country governed its federal-provincial fiscal relations up until fairly recently was derived from the report. The essence of the 1941 Dominion-provincial tax arrangements provided that the provinces would relinquish personal income and corporation taxes, along with succession duties, in return for which they would receive carefully worked out sums of money from the federal government.

In 1962 a new scheme for regulating the tax relations of the federal and provincial governments was evolved. This new approach was centred on the notion that the federal government would act as a tax collection agency for the provincial governments, on the understanding that the provincial tax base would be similar to that of the federal government. Furthermore, it was arranged that these taxes would be collected free by the federal government on behalf of the provinces, as an added inducement to allowing the federal government to act as a tax collector. The federal government would then hand over to the provincial governments their agreed-upon share of tax money collected.

The central question, however, which has dominated Canadian fiscal relationships since Confederation is the problem of ascertaining what proportion of the Canadian taxpayer's dollar would accrue to which government. At the time of Confederation it was quite logical that, since the federal government had most of the legislative authority, it should have most of the nation's revenue. Since 1867, however, a whole sequence of events, including the decisions handed down by the Privy Council, have greatly enhanced the legislative jurisdiction and responsibilities of the provinces. Not only did the courts bestow on the provincial legislatures powers not contemplated by the Fathers of Confederation, but in addition such matters as education, originally given to the provinces by the British North America Act, have become considerably more expensive than anyone could have possibly imagined in 1867. No one then could have been expected to foresee that Canada's provinces would spend hundreds of millions of dollars annually on higher education alone. Similarly, it was impossible to foresee the kind of burden that would be placed on provincial governments by the need to build modern highways and to develop substantial welfare schemes. The heavy responsibilities faced by provincial governments have made them desperate for more revenue. On the other hand, the central government has had to carry the financial weight of fighting two world wars and meeting the problems posed by a major depression in the thirties. In addition, federal authorities realize that the responsibility for the monetary and fiscal stability of the nation rests with the central government, and that it must, at all times, if it is to regulate the national economy, have a high degree of control over both the raising and spending of funds in Canada. During the Second World War the resolution of these problems was not exceptionally difficult in that the majority of Canadians agreed that the primary aim of the nation must be to win the war. It therefore became almost unpatriotic for the provinces to demand funds. They entered Dominion-provincial negotiations during the early part of the war in a weak bargaining position, and thus they accepted the federal tax rental proposals of 1941.

After the war, the resurgent nationalism of French Canada, combined with increased demands made on the provincial governments by their constituents, prompted new provincial tax demands. Until the issues raised by the federal-provincial conferences on the Constitution from 1968 to 1971, this struggle over tax resources was probably the most important political and constitutional question in Canada. In any reformulation of the Constitution this question of tax allocations will probably loom as one of the most controversial problems. Since the division of tax resources is, in fact, decided at the federal-provincial conferences, with the respective legislatures really only adding a pro-forma implementation of the agreements reached in that forum, it is apparent why this part of our constitutional process is so important, even though no reference is made to it in the British North America Act. It now seems that all important constitutional issues will be placed before various federal-provincial conferences, either at the Attorney-General or the Prime Minister and Premiers level.

Another institution of considerable interest is the provincial Premiers' Conference. While at the time of the writing of the first edition of this book it appeared that this institution would become one of increasing political importance, events since 1969 have not justified this view.

It is fortunate that the provinces have a substantial amount of legislative authority and the fiscal strength. This allows for government which is closer to the people on matters of local concern, and for legislative experimentation in different areas of the country. We have in Canada a good balance between federal and provincial responsibility, and this accord should not be changed lightly. Much of the credit for maintaining this delicate balance between the federal and provincial spheres is attributable to the effectiveness of the machinery which has been devised to allow them to communicate with each other.

REFERENCES

1. D. V. Smiley, *Canada in Question: Federalism in the Seventies*, McGraw-Hill Ryerson Limited, Toronto, 1972.
2. Richard Simeon, *Federal-Provincial Diplomacy: The Making of Recent Policy in Canada*, University of Toronto Press, Toronto, 1972.
3. See J. R. Mallory, *The Structure of Canadian Government*, Macmillan Company of Canada Limited, Toronto, 1971. See also J. Stefan Dupre, David M. Cameron, Graeme H. McKechnie and Theodore B. Rotenberg, *Federalism: Policy Development*, University of Toronto Press, Toronto, 1973.
4. E. Gallant, "The Machinery of Federal Provincial Relations: I," *Canadian Public Administration*, vol. 8, no. 4 (December 1965), p. 515.
5. E. Gallant, "The Machinery of Federal Provincial Relations: I," p. 515.
6. See E. Gallant, "The Machinery of Federal Provincial Relations: I," pp. 520-1.
7. E. Gallant, "The Machinery of Federal Provincial Relations: I," p. 529.
8. E. Gallant, "The Machinery of Federal Provincial Relations: I," p. 524.
9. R. M. Burns, "The Machinery of Federal Provincial Relations: II," *Canadian Public Administration*, vol. 8, no. 4, (December 1965), p. 532.
10. R. M. Burns, "The Machinery of Federal Provincial Relations: II," p. 537.
11. An exhaustive study of this subject can be found in a work prepared for the Canadian Tax Foundation by A. M. Moore, J. H. Perry and D. I. Beach, *The Financing of Canadian Federation*, Canadian Tax Foundation, Toronto, 1966.
    See also R. M. Dawson, *The Government of Canada*, 5th ed. University of Toronto Press, Toronto, 1970, pp. 99-118.
12. See A. M. Moore, J. H. Perry and D. I. Beach, *The Financing of Canadian Federation*, pp. 1-15.

Seven

Constitutional Change
and Constitutional Goals

At the time of the first edition of this book, which appeared in 1969, the process of constitutional review was in full flight. The culmination of this process was the Canadian Constitutional Charter, usually referred to as the Victoria Charter, which emerged at the end of a series of federal-provincial conferences running from February 1968 to June 1971. The history of these conferences has now been succinctly summarized by Professor Smiley[1] and, accordingly, do not have to be documented here. The Victoria Charter, however, is a document of considerable interest and will be referred to frequently during the course of this chapter. In essence, the Charter provided for an entrenched constitutional document replacing much of the present constitutional framework. It was not regarded, however, as the final constitutional document as further areas of the Constitution were to be reviewed and changed if it was deemed necessary. The Charter itself was divided into ten parts, the most important of which involved political rights, language rights, the Supreme Court of Canada and an amendment formula. The most significant impact of the Charter would probably have been felt through the entrenchment of political rights. This would probably have accelerated any tendency towards a more activist judiciary, although the impact of the courts might have been somewhat less predictable in view of the complicated machinery for substantial provincial involvement in the appointment of judges to the Supreme Court of Canada. In any event prolonged speculation about the impact that the Charter would have had is of little value because of its rejection by the province of Quebec. Thus, constitutional change since 1969 has come about as a result of the usual evolutionary process, rather than the battering ram of a wholly new constitutional document.

It is interesting to reflect upon the near hysteria generated to promote the drafting of a new constitution. Dire predictions of almost immediate dissolution of Confederation if a new constitution was not quickly adopted now seem ludicrous. The arguments for the immediate adoption of a new constitution struck the original writer of this book as vastly exaggerated and misleading, and we feel that some of the original arguments against the drive for a new constitution outlined in the first edition are still valid and bear repeating.

The urge for certainty is undoubtedly a strong motivating factor among some proponents of a new constitution. The desire to resolve uncertainties by drafting a comprehensive code is a familiar social phenomenon in man's history. Wiping the slate clean and starting again always seems rather refreshing, as it appeals to one's urge to tidy things up and one always hopes it will bring the kind of satisfaction one gets from cleaning the top of a cluttered desk. We do not advocate a total absence of constitutional change, as this would obviously be futile. It is trite to underline the inevitability of change, but it is none the less a basic factor in all constitutional analysis. The question, thus, is not whether one is for or against constitutional change, but how such change is to come about, how far it should go, and what direction it should take.

It is common for critics of the existing Constitution to underline the fact that the British North America Act was passed in 1867. Their thesis seems to be that, since the document is now over a hundred years old, it thus must be out of date and should be scrapped. The fact that the United States Constitution is almost twice as old and yet still serves that country more than adequately is totally ignored. Secondly, the fact that the British North America Act is only one small part of our constitutional structure is rarely mentioned. When these would-be constitution drafters talk of a new constitution they almost invariably focus on the British North America Act, but fail to indicate whether they are also interested in abandoning or changing the vast portion of our Constitution which is unwritten and based on convention. Leaving aside the division of legislative powers, the most important parts of our constitutional structure, such as the cabinet system and the parliamentary process generally, are not substantially influenced by the terms of the British North America Act. Thus, when one is discussing the Constitution, it must be remembered that this does not refer exclusively to the British North America Act, but to that complex multitude of statutes, judicial decisions and constitutional conventions which intertwine in a complex fabric to produce the constitutional system of this country.[2]

The existing structure has proved very responsive to national needs. Canada has, under the existing Constitution, adjusted to and met the demands of two world wars and several economic depressions, and so far has survived the stresses resulting from the bicultural nature of the country. The Constitution has proved sufficiently flexible to permit massive centralization of power during war time in order to meet the nation's military responsibilities, yet it has not proved a hindrance to recent decentralist trends. If we have failed to resolve social and political problems, that has been the fault of men in authority and not due to any flaw in the constitutional mechanism. In fact, it is our view that the Constitution has proved to be infinitely more flexible in dealing with our national problems than has the more formalized constitutional structure of the United States. Unfortunately, flexibility must inevitably breed a certain degree of uncertainty and, as Jerome Frank pointed out in his book *Law and the Modern Mind*,[3] man, for complex psychological reasons, has a deep-rooted need for certainty. Frank emphasized, however, that most of this urgent need for certainty has neurotic roots and is an unattainable goal anyway.

One of the contemporary issues testing the viability of the Constitution is that of federal or provincial control of natural resources, particularly with respect to petroleum and natural gas. At the time of writing, this issue has been underlined by the introduction in Parliament of the Petroleum Administration Act. This bill provides that in the absence of federal-provincial agreement the federal Cabinet may determine the maximum price at which a provincially owned or regulated company may charge for petroleum or natural gas beyond its borders. This would mean that Alberta and other producer provinces would have to sell at a federally designated price, rather than at a price determined by the international market. This would likely have the effect of producer provinces selling their irreplaceable natural resources at a price lower than could otherwise be obtained. The producer provinces argue that this amounts to subsidization of the industrialized regions of Canada to their detriment. They further argue that the effect of this attempted control by the federal Parliament would be to diminish their constitutional right to control "All Lands, Mines, Minerals, and Royalties" vested in them by virtue of Section 109 of the B.N.A. Act, 1867, which was made applicable to the western provinces by the B.N.A. Act, 1930. To date these issues have not been resolved by the courts, but a judicial ruling with respect to them seems highly likely to be made in the near future. The issue is a vital one, because if the federal Parliament can, in essence, determine the price of domestic distribution of provincially owned natural resources, the legislative and economic position of the provinces will be dramatically weakened.

Critics of the existing Constitution often tend to underestimate the extent of constitutional change since 1867. In order to respond to the various crises previously mentioned, it has been undergoing continual change. Since Confederation many significant alterations have occurred. Appeals to the Judicial Committee of the Privy Council have been abolished and replaced by appeals to the Supreme Court, now the final judicial arbiter for Canada. There has been effective discontinuance of the utilization of the disallowance power, both by the monarch and by the central government in Ottawa. The British North America Act has been amended to allow large portions of this Act to be changed by the federal Parliament alone. We have witnessed new areas of jurisdiction being undertaken by the two major areas of government, federal and provincial. There has been a much greater use of the French language within the ranks of the federal bureaucracy. The Official Languages Act[4] has been enacted and its constitutional validity has been upheld by the Supreme Court of Canada.[5] We have seen considerable flexibility in the allocation and spending of tax monies by both the federal and provincial governments. There have been dramatic alterations in our party system, which has been changed, federally, from the traditional two-party system to one composed of four federal political parties, and provincially, by the emergence of such parties as the Social Credit Party, the Union Nationale and the Parti Québecois. We have witnessed provinces playing a role in the formation of international agreements, a fact obviously not contemplated in 1867. This is a chronicling of just a few of the many changes that have taken place in our constitutional and political systems since Confederation. The Constitution, in fact, is continually being readjusted to meet existing needs. It is this capacity of our system to adjust to changing needs that is the most eloquent testimony to its flexibility and viability.

In discussions respecting constitutional change probably no area has been more discussed than that of finding a suitable amendment formula for the British North America Act. In fact in late 1974 the Prime Minister of Canada indicated that during the course of the next four or five years another attempt would be made to devise a purely domestic amendment formula. Though the terms of the British North America Act were decided upon by Canadians, its formal enactment was, and continues to be by the British Parliament. Thus, no provisions were contained in the statute for its amendment because, being a British statute, it could be amended, like any other British statute, by Act of Parliament. As has been described earlier in this book, however, there are provisions within the British North America Act for changes of certain of its terms by the Canadian Parliament,[6] and by the provincial legislatures.[7] For the most part, though, it was recognized that, except where specifically provided, the British North America Act would have to be amended by the British Parliament. A subsequent modification of this principle was made in 1949, with the passage of the British North America Act 1949 (2). This amendment, now known as Section 91 (1), allows for the amendment of the British North America Act by the federal Parliament, except with respect to sections of the Act dealing with five areas. With respect to these matters amendment must be by a statute of the British Parliament. These entrenched portions of the British North America Act include matters conferred on the provinces, which means that no change in the division of federal-provincial power can be made unilaterally by the federal Parliament. In addition, Section 91(1) entrenches any portions of the British North America Act dealing with schools, the use of the English and French languages, and requirements that there be a session of Parliament once each year and that no House of Commons shall continue for more than five years. This means that, with respect to the most important part of the British North America Act, namely, the division of legislative powers, change can only be brought about by resort to British parliamentary action.

There have been reasonably frequent amendments of the British North America Act by the British Parliament. There has, however, grown up around these formal legal actions by the British Parliament a whole sequence of constitutional conventions. First is the one that no action will ever be taken by the United Kingdom Parliament without formal request from Canada. Secondly, it has evolved that Canadian parliamentary approval is obtained prior to sending a request from the Canadian government to the British Parliament for action. Thirdly, no amendment is ever made to the Canadian Constitution at the request of a Canadian province only. Finally, the Canadian Parliament generally will not request an amendment affecting federal-provincial power without prior consultation with and agreement of the province or provinces concerned.[8] These latter principles are, of course, constitutional conventions and have not been written into positive law; however, they are so deeply embodied in our constitutional system that, short of a total breakdown in the constitutional process, it is impossible to imagine them being ignored.

Changes in the British North America Act itself however, are only one small way in which constitutional change has been effected in Canada. Large portions of our Constitution are made up of federal and provincial statutes, which can be amended by the federal or provincial legislature concerned. Under the terms of Section 92 (1) a provincial legislature is given complete authority to change its constitution in any respect, except as regards the office of Lieutenant-Governor. Similarly, leaving aside the questions of a House of Commons session being held every year and of no House of Commons lasting for more than five years, the federal Parliament is authorized to make virtually any change it wishes to make with respect to its constitutional functioning, without resort to the Parliament of the United Kingdom. For example, the terms of the Supreme Court of Canada Act can be changed, at any time, by the federal Parliament. However, to consider only these formal aspects of constitutional amendment is to ignore the underlying realities of political and social change in Canada. In fact, the workings of our constitutional system are so deeply ingrained in our national culture that widespread changes in our system would require a substantial element of popular support. This tenuous relationship between positive legal power and the effective living law of the community is one of the most interesting features of our system. A simple technical capacity for change is combined with the protections provided by sociological solidarity and restraint. It is interesting to look at provincial constitutions, all portions of which by clear statutory enactment, are amendable by the provincial legislatures, except for the office of Lieutenant-Governor, and to find, nevertheless, that the systems are virtually identical from one province to another. It is our view that widespread change has never been effected because it has not been necessary. Our provincial governments have operated smoothly and effectively under a parliamentary system. They have generally adapted to social needs, and this system has, at the same time, provided for political stability. There is no doubt that, under this arrangement, the provincial legislatures have been rather weak in comparison with the executive, but this is preferable to the American system where the governor of a state is, in many instances, impotent to cope with an excessively powerful group of very independent legislators.

There have been widespread demands for changes in many areas of the Canadian constitutional system but it is our intention to focus, in this concluding chapter, on three particularly interesting constitutional topics: constitutional amendment,[9] the protection of civil liberties, and some of the questions surrounding the negotiation and implementation of treaties. These are not the only sensitive areas of the Constitution, and one other particularly significant area, namely the Supreme Court, has already been discussed earlier in considerable detail.

Perhaps no other area of our constitutional system has been more discussed and analysed by the central and provincial governments than that of constitutional amendment. The reason for this is that it is still necessary to obtain formal statutory action by the British Parliament, in order to change large segments of the British North America Act. Many argue that it is humiliating that Canada should have to seek parliamentary approval from another country to change parts of its Constitution. Prior to the emergence of the Victoria Charter, no less than five federal-provincial conferences, from 1927 through to 1964, focused on the problem of finding an amending formula that did not require recourse to the British Parliament. It seemed as if success had finally been achieved when in 1964, the representatives of the federal and provincial governments finally agreed on what came to be commonly known as the Fulton-Favreau formula. This was the first time that all parties had unanimously agreed on a purely domestic amending scheme. However, these hopes were to be short-lived, because, shortly after the 1964 conference, the Quebec government reversed its position and rejected the formula.

There is no need at this time to examine in detail all the provisions of the Fulton-Favreau formula, as this has already been done.[10] Put very briefly, the Fulton-Favreau formula gave the Parliament of Canada sole authority to amend the Canadian Constitution, subject in certain instances, to approval of some or all of the provinces, depending on which portion of the Constitution was to be amended. For example, matters dealing with the powers of the provinces, the rights and privileges of the provinces, provincial assets, the use of the English or French language, or the relationship between the number of members of the House and the number of senators, were all subject to the unanimity rule. This meant that any changes in the British North America Act dealing with any of these subjects could only be brought about by the federal Parliament with the unanimous consent of the legislatures of all of the provinces. Similarly, provisions dealing with another touchy subject, education, could only be changed with the unanimous consent of all of the provinces except Newfoundland, and special arrangements were made for that province.

Since the formula did not easily facilitate amendments, the latter part of the formula provided a scheme whereby delegation was permitted between the federal Parliament and the provincial legislatures and vice versa. Inter-delegation between provincial and federal legislative spheres had been declared unconstitutional in the Nova Scotia case,[11] and thus the latter part of the Fulton-Favreau formula was intended not only to obliterate the effect of this case, but to also provide flexibility in the formula to counterbalance the rigidity of requiring provincial unanimity with respect to so many areas of the Constitution.

As already stated, the most recent purely domestic amendment formula was that contained on Part IX of the Victoria Charter, the main provision of which was Article 49 which provided that:

> Amendments to the Constitution of Canada may from time to time be made by proclamation issued by the Governor-General under the Great Seal of Canada when so authorized by resolutions of the Senate and House of Commons and of the Legislative Assemblies of at least a majority of the Provinces that includes:
>
> (1) every Province that at any time before the issue of such proclamation had, according to any previous general census, a population of at least twenty-five percent of the population of Canada;
> (2) at least two of the Atlantic Provinces;
> (3) at least two of the Western Provinces that have, according to the then latest general census, combined populations of at least fifty percent of the population of all the Western Provinces.

Articles 53 and 54 provided that the federal Parliament and provincial legislatures could unilaterally amend their respective constitutions. These general powers were qualified, however, with respect to certain fundamental rights, privileges and institutions. With respect to these it was provided that the formula set out in Article 49 must be utilized to effect an amendment. The rights, privileges and institutions which must be amended through the utilization of Article 49 are set out in Article 55, as follows:

> (1) the office of the Queen, of the Governor General and of the Lieutenant-Governor;
> (2) the requirements of the Constitution of Canada respecting yearly sessions of the Parliament of Canada and the Legislatures;
> (3) the maximum period fixed by the Constitution of Canada for the duration of the House of Commons and the Legislative Assemblies;
> (4) the powers of the Senate;
> (5) the number of members by which a Province is entitled to be represented in the Senate and the residence qualifications of Senators;
> (6) the right of a Province to a number of members in the House of Commons not less than the number of Senators representing the Province;
> (7) the principles of proportionate representation of the Provinces in the House of Commons prescribed by the Constitution of Canada; and
> (8) except as provided in Article 16, the requirements of this Charter respecting the use of the English or French language.

This amendment formula was endorsed by the Special Joint Committee of the Senate and House of Commons on the Constitution of Canada, and probably will be the starting point of the continuing search, announced by the Prime Minister of Canada in late 1974, to find a new amendment formula. The amendment process contained in the Victoria Charter, while not perfect, is at least less complex and more flexible than the Fulton-Favreau formula which, in certain instances, required the consent of the federal Parliament and all ten provincial legislatures.

Another sensitive constitutional area is the problem of treaty negotiation and implementation.[12] Quebec, in particular, has felt that it should be permitted to negotiate international agreements that touch upon subjects under provincial control. The result has been that Quebec negotiated a cultural agreement with France, though face-saving arrangements were made so that the agreement ultimately was under the umbrella of the Ottawa government. Similarly, British Columbia played a substantial role in the negotiations of the Columbia River Treaty, though formal signing of this international agreement was done under the auspices of the central government. The central issue, however, is whether provinces can unilaterally, without benefit of federal intervention, undertake to carry out all aspects of making international agreements.

The terms of the British North America Act dealing with treaties are unsatisfactory, because they relate to a political situation which no longer exists. By virtue of Section 132 of the British North America Act, the only section dealing with the treaty problem, "The Parliament and Government of Canada" are given all the necessary powers for "performing the Obligations of Canada or of any Province thereof, as Part of the British Empire, towards Foreign Countries, arising under Treaties between the Empire and such Foreign Countries." Thus, by virtue of Section 132, Canada could implement by domestic legislation any British Empire treaty.

Section 132 thereby gave to the federal Parliament the power to pass legislation giving domestic legal effect to any treaty signed by Canada as part of the British Empire. It perhaps should be noted that the mere signing of a treaty does not, in Canada, make the terms of that treaty lawfully binding within the borders of the country. For a treaty to have legal effect domestically there must be a domestic statute passed. Section 132 is illustrative, once again, of the intention of the Fathers of Confederation to place the central government in a powerful position. It, in effect, allows Parliament to legislate on matters of purely provincial jurisdiction, subject only to the condition that the legislation is carrying out the obligations of Canada under the terms of a British Empire treaty.

The right to conclude international agreements, as distinguished from their implementation, is part of the royal prerogative. This means that treaties can be signed by the Governor General in Canada's name, acting, of course, on the advice of the government, especially the Secretary of State for External Affairs. Some proponents of increased provincial authority have argued that, since the Lieutenant-Governor is possessed of prerogative power, this includes the right to enter into treaties with foreign states on matters under provincial legislative control. This argument, however, is difficult to sustain as a matter of technical legal analysis, and has disastrous implications for Canada from a policy point of view.

The treaty provisions of the Constitution made sense at the time of Confederation, because in 1867 all Canadian treaties were made under the auspices of the Empire. However, as Canada emerged as a separate international signatory, Section 132, if read literally, was legal deadwood. The question for the courts to decide was whether Section 132 should be interpreted in accordance with Canada's new status as a separate international signatory to international agreements. As this subject has been well studied, it is unnecessary to recapitulate fully the judicial reasoning with respect to this issue. [13]

It is sufficient for our purposes to examine briefly the effect of the most important case on the treaty power in Canada, namely *Attorney-General for Canada v. Attorney-General for Ontario*. [14] The Privy Council decided that Section 132 was to have a restrictive interpretation, that is to say, Canada was not to have the benefit of Section 132 unless the treaty was actually a British Empire treaty. Thus, the court, in effect, held that the signing of international agreements was a federal responsibility, but that the power to domestically implement the treaty was determined by the division of legislative powers. Thus, if the federal government signs an international treaty dealing with a matter within its normal legislative jurisdiction, then it has the responsibility for passing a statute to give domestic legal effect to the treaty. If the central government, however, negotiates a treaty dealing with a provincial matter, then only the provinces can give domestic legal effect to that treaty. There was a suggestion by three of the judges in the case of *Johannesson v. West St. Paul* that Section 132 could be given a living tree interpretation; however, the court was divided on this question and the case was basically decided on other grounds. [15] Therefore, it seems that the Labour Conventions case is the determinate one with respect to treaty implementation. Furthermore, it is a decision which probably coincides with political realities in Canada. Probably very few things would provoke Quebec more than the proposition that, merely by signing an international agreement on a provincial subject, the federal Parliament would be given authority to legislate in that area. The real question is that of the role of provincial governments in the negotiation of international agreements.

The provinces have already entered into administrative arrangements with foreign governments, such as Quebec's educational and cultural entente with France. [16] The provinces have not, however, been accorded international status. This is an issue on which the federal government can be expected to take a hard line. As the White Paper on international relations suggests, the provinces probably should have an increased consultative role with respect to certain agreements Canada is negotiating. [17] The White Paper suggests that there should be federal-provincial talks respecting what treaties should be negotiated and implemented. At the same time, it is suggested that there be provincial participation at many of the conferences and meetings, when

Canada is negotiating international agreements.[18]

A third area of continuing concern is that of civil liberties.[19] The Victoria Charter provided for the entrenchment of certain political rights, outlined in Part I of the Charter. Article 1 states that all persons have "the following fundamental freedoms:

freedom of thought, conscience and religion,
freedom of opinion and expression, and
freedom of peaceful assembly and of association;

and all laws shall be construed and applied so as not to abrogate or abridge any such freedom." Other articles in the Charter were designed to ensure universal suffrage and free democratic elections to the House of Commons and provincial legislative assemblies. The rest of Part I provided that the House of Commons and provincial legislative assemblies should not continue without elections for more than five years, except during wartime, when by special procedures their lifetimes could be extended. The Charter further provided that the federal Parliament and provincial legislatures should sit at least once each year. The aforementioned rights are all in fact presently protected in various statutes, such as the B.N.A. Act, 1867, the Bill of Rights, and numerous provincial statutes. The effect of the Charter would have been to place these rights beyond ordinary legislative control.

Although the question is now academic because of its rejection, the deliberations which led up to the drafting of the Charter provoked considerable debate. The argument against entrenchment has been eloquently stated by two prominent scholars, D. Smiley[20] and D. Schmeiser.[21] The essence of their argument is that entrenchment would be an invitation to the courts to emulate in Canada a role similar to that of the courts in the United States. Dean Schmeiser objects to turning over to the courts fundamental questions of public policy, often thus frustrating the will of popularly elected legislators. He accurately sees the American model of judicial review as undemocratic, in that it involves substituting the views of appointed judges for those of the democratically elected assemblies. He sees the main benefactors of extended judicial review, the result of entrenchment, as being the legal profession. He refers to the thousands of cases in the United States which were argued in the courts on the basis of alleged constitutional invalidity, many of them frivolous, expensive and time consuming. Schmeiser very aptly puts the question: Why would Canada want to reject a system that is working reasonably well for the system in the United States which has demonstrated itself to be in many ways inferior to that in Canada?

Canadian legislatures, both federally and provincially, have enacted a considerable amount of legislation in the field of human rights. For example, federally there has been the Canadian Bill of Rights and the Canada Fair Employment Practices Act. Ontario has passed The Ontario Human Rights Code, The Age Discrimination Act, and The Freedom of Worship Act. Saskatchewan has passed The Saskatchewan Bill of Rights Act, a Fair Employment Practices Act and a Fair Accommodation Practices Act. British Columbia has passed The

Human Rights Act. Every province has some legislation designed to protect human rights.[22] This reflects the legislators' attitude to and, in turn, the public's concern for human rights. It is ultimately the populace's attitude toward civil liberties which is important, because no amount of legal machinery will protect a nation from political autocracy if its inclination is strongly in that direction.

Since the first edition of this book there have been several major developments with respect to civil liberties. First, there are the two landmark decisions of the Supreme Court of Canada, the Drybones[23] and Lavell[24] cases. It is unnecessary to recite the details with respect to these cases as this has already been done in Chapter Three. Briefly, however, the Lavell case returned to the pre-Drybones position that specific provisions of a federal statute take precedence over the more general words of the federal Bill of Rights.

Secondly, there have been dramatic developments in the area of language rights. The federal Parliament passed in 1969 The Official Languages Act,[25] which, in essence, declared that English and French are the official languages of Canada. The statute provides in Section 2 that they "possess and enjoy equality of status and equal rights and privileges as to their use in all the institutions of the Parliament and Government of Canada." The constitutionality of the Act was challenged and upheld by the Supreme Court of Canada in *Jones v. The Attorney-General of Canada et al.*[26] In essence, the Supreme Court upheld the legislation as being a valid exercise of the federal Parliament's jurisdiction to "make Laws for the Peace, Order and good Government of Canada." Further, those provisions of the Act relating to the courts were upheld by utilizing Sections 91(27) and 101 of the B.N.A. Act. Another event of major political consequence with respect to language was the passage in 1974 by the Quebec National Assembly of the Official Language Act, usually referred to as Bill 22. This statute provides in Section 1 that "French is the official language of the province of Quebec." The statute then proceeds to make various provisions with respect to the exclusive use, priority of and protection of the French language. For example, all texts and documents emanating from the Quebec government must be in French, though they "may be accompanied by an English version" (Section 8). The Act further provides that French "is the language of internal communication in the public administration (Section 12). All government contracts must be in French (Section 17), and all members of professional societies must have a working knowledge of the French language in accordance with standards determined by regulations of the Lieutenant-Governor-in-Council (Section 21). In the realm of business, firm names must be in French (Section 30), and French is to be the only language of labour relations (Section 25). There are some controversial provisions with respect to education, but the one most likely to provoke resentment among non-English and non-French immigrants is Section 41 which provides that:

> Pupils must have a sufficient knowledge of the language of instruction to receive their instruction in that language.

> Pupils who do not have a sufficient knowledge of any of the languages of instruction must receive their instruction in French.

There seems little doubt that there will be litigation over the legality of this statute, and more particularly, specific provisions of it. It is probably with respect to the sections concerning education that the most serious questions will arise.

The final event of major significance with respect to civil liberties since the first edition of this book was the proclamation by the Governor General-in-Council in October 16, 1970, of the War Measures Act.[27] The occasion for this very extreme action was the kidnapping of Quebec Labour Minister, Pierre Laporte and British Trade Commissioner, James Cross, by members of an extremist separatist group known as Le Front de Libération du Québec. This was the first time that the Act had ever been proclaimed in peacetime, although it had been widely used in both the First and Second World Wars, as has been described earlier in this book. The regulations passed by the Governor General-in-Council under the authority of this Act, though considerably less sweeping than those passed during either of the two world wars, provided for a definite break with usual legal practices in Canada.

The regulations provided that the F.L.Q. was an unlawful association and that membership in or support of it was an offence punishable by imprisonment for a period of up to five years. The regulations also provided for stiff penalties for knowingly assisting persons in the F.L.Q. or providing accommodation for the organization. The regulations further gave the authorities special powers of search and detention of persons arrested for alleged violation of the regulations. Parliament in November 1970 passed the Public Order (Temporary Measures) Act, 1970,[28] to come into effect immediately upon deproclamation of the War Measures Act. Essentially, this statute continued the provisions of the October regulations, but in a somewhat softened and more limited manner. It is interesting to note, however, that like the War Measures Act it was specifically declared in section 12 to "operate notwithstanding the Canadian Bill of Rights." The Act did provide for a specific date of expiration, subject to its being terminated earlier by proclamation of the Governor General-in-Council.

Very few, if any, events in Canadian history have provoked so much critical debate as the proclamation of the War Measures Act in 1970. A whole series of newspaper comments, academic articles and various types of books debated whether or not the federal government's action was justified.[29] It even prompted a government minister, Gérard Pelletier, to write a book defending the government's position.[30] Public opinion polls and the overwhelming majority of members of Parliament, however, supported the measure. It is interesting to note, however, that Robert Stanfield, the Progressive Conservative leader of the Opposition in October 1970 stated in January 1975 that, in retrospect, he is sorry that he supported the government's extreme action at the time of the crisis.

Viewed from the perspective of utility, the government's action was successful to the extent that there have been no major outbreaks of separatist violence or terrorism since the October crisis. It has the effect of completely channeling separatist activities into traditional political channels. Viewed in hindsight, it is hard to say that there existed the "war, invasion, or insurrection, real or apprehended" required for the proclamation of the War Measures Act. There seems to be little doubt, however, that the government was justified in taking the position that it needed some special temporary powers, but the fact remains that these could probably have been obtained by the quick passage by Parliament of a special powers act designed specifically to deal with the F.L.Q. crisis.

The mania of the sixties has been replaced by the sobriety of the seventies. In the late nineteen sixties all things seemed possible, even the adoption of a new constitution for Canada, whether needed or not. Those naive expectations were dashed with the rejection by Quebec of the Victoria Charter. Prime Minister Trudeau, however, announced late in 1974 that there would be another attempt over the next five years to find a purely domestic amending formula, despite six previous failures to achieve this objective. It seems a realistic expectation that this objective will be achieved by 1980. It is unlikely, however, that even if this objective is achieved that widespread changes in the Constitution will result because, as in the past, it will be the lack of political consensus that will probably forestall formal legal amendment rather than technical legal difficulties. In terms of legal technicalities the present Constitution is exceptionally easy to amend, but political factors have forestalled anything but minimal recourse to formal amendment. Irrespective, however, of formal amendment the Constitution will continue to change and adapt to new conditions. A constitution is more than a basic document, it is also a whole structure of statutes, judicial decisions, conventions and political relationships always adapting and adjusting to new realities.

REFERENCES

1. D.V. Smiley, *Canada in Question: Federalism in the Seventies*, McGraw-Hill Ryerson Limited, Toronto, 1972.
2. Two interesting articles commenting on one hundred years of constitutionalism in Canada have been written by B. Laskin, "Reflections on the Canadian Constitution after the First Century," *The Canadian Bar Review*, vol. 45, no. 3 (September 1967), p. 395, and G. E. LeDain, "Reflections on the Canadian Constitution after the First Century," *The Canadian Bar Review*, vol. 45, no. 3 (September 1967), p. 402.
   See also an interesting survey of this subject by D.V. Smiley, *The Canadian Political Nationality*, Methuen, Toronto, 1967.
3. Jerome Frank, *Law and the Modern Mind*, Doubleday & Company Inc., Garden City, 1963.
4. Official Languages Act, R.S.C. 1970, C.0-2.
5. *Jones v. Attorney-General of Canada et al.*, 45 D.L.R. (3d) 583.
6. Ss. 35, 41 and 47.
7. Ss. 78, 83 and 84.

8. G. Favreau, *The Amendment of the Constitution of Canada*, Queen's Printer, Ottawa, 1965, p. 15. This document was sponsored by the Canadian government and published under the name of the then Minister of Justice, Mr. Guy Favreau.
9. The amendment process is fully described in two works: P. Gérin-Lajoie, *Constitutional Amendment in Canada*, University of Toronto Press, Toronto, 1950; and G. Favreau, *The Amendment of the Constitution of Canada*, Queen's Printer, Ottawa, 1965.
10. See G. Favreau, *The Amendment of the Constitution of Canada*, pp. 32-53. E.R. Alexander, "A Constitutional Strait Jacket for Canada," *The Canadian Bar Review*, vol. 43, no. 2 (May 1965), p. 262.
11. *Attorney-General for Nova Scotia v. Attorney-General for Canada*, [1951] S.C.R. 31. It is respectfully submitted that this case was wrongly decided in terms of both policy and logical application of the existing rules of constitutional law. The arguments of the dissenting judge of the Nova Scotia Court of Appeal, Mr. Justice Doull, are, in our opinion, sound.
12. G.L. Morris, "The Treaty-Making Power: A Canadian Dilemma," *The Canadian Bar Review*, vol. 45, no. 3 (September 1967) p. 478.
   For a comparison of the treaty power in Canada with that of another federal state see R. Cheffins, "The Negotiation, Ratification and Implementation of Treaties in Canada and Australia: Part I," *The Alberta Law Review*, no. 4 (Fall 1958), p. 312, and R. Cheffins, "The Negotiation, Ratification and Implementation of Treaties in Canada and Australia: Part II," *The Alberta Law Review*, no. 5 (Spring 1960), p. 410.
   See also Richard H. Leach, Donald E. Walker and Thomas Allen Levy, "Province-State trans-border relations: a preliminary assessment," *Canadian Public Administration*, vol. 16, no. 3, 1973, p. 468; and Gerald L. Morris, "Canadian Federalism and International Law," *Canadian Perspectives on International Law and Organization*, R. St.J. Macdonald, Gerald L. Morris and Douglas M. Johnston, eds., University of Toronto Press, Toronto, 1974, p. 55.
13. P. Martin, *Federalism and International Relations*, pp. 24-5. R. Cheffins, "The Negotiation, Ratification and Implementation of Treaties in Canada and Australia: Part II," *The Alberta Law Review*, no. 5 (Spring 1960), pp. 420-8.
   N.A.M. MacKenzie, "Canada and the Treaty-making Power," *Canadian Bar Review*, vol. 15, no. 6, p. 453.
   F.P. Barcoe, *The Constitution of Canada*, The Carswell Co., Toronto, 1965, pp. 178-85.
14. Usually referred to as the Labour Conventions case, *Attorney-General for Canada v. Attorney-General for Ontario* [1937] A.C. 327.
15. *Johannesson v. West St. Paul* [1952] 1 S.C.R. 292.
16. P. Martin, *Federalism and International Relations*, Queen's Printer, Ottawa, 1968, pp. 26-27.
17. P. Martin, *Federalism and International Relations*, Queen's Printer, Ottawa, 1968, p. 44.
18. See also Gerald L. Morris, "Canadian Federalism and International Law," *Canadian Perspectives on International Law and Organization*, R. St.J. Macdonald, Gerald L. Morris and Douglas M. Johnston, eds., University of Toronto Press, Toronto, 1974, pp. 63-8.
19. D.A. Schmeiser, *Civil Liberties in Canada*, Oxford University Press, London, 1964. F.R. Scott, *Civil Liberties and Canadian Federalism*, University of Toronto Press, Toronto, 1959.
   W.S. Tarnopolsky, *The Canadian Bill of Rights*, 2nd ed., The Carswell Co., Toronto, 1975.
20. Donald V. Smiley, "The Case Against The Canadian Charter of Human Rights," *Politics: Canada*, Paul Fox ed., 3rd ed., McGraw-Hill Company of Canada Limited, Toronto, 1970, p. 484.
21. Douglas A. Schmeiser, "The Case Against Entrenchment of a Canadian Bill of Rights," *Dalhousie Law Journal*, vol. 1, no. 1, (September 1973).
22. For a list of the main Canadian statutes protecting human rights passed in 1969 see P.E. Trudeau, *A Canadian Charter of Human Rights*, pp. 171-4.
23. (1969) D.L.R. (3d) 473.

24. (1974) 38 D.L.R. (3d) 481.
25. R.S.C., 1970, C.0-2.
26. (1974) 45 D.L.R. (3d) 583.
27. R.S.C., 1970, C. W-2.
28. S.C., 1970, C.2.
29. Brian Moore, *The Revolution Script*, McClelland and Stewart, Toronto, 1971.
    Ron Haggart and Aubrey E. Golden, *Rumours of War*, New Press, Toronto, 1971.
    Abrahim Rotstein, ed., *Power Corrupted: the October crisis and the Repression of Quebec*, New Press, Toronto, 1971.
    Dennis Smith, *Bleeding Hearts . . . Bleeding Country: Canada and the Quebec Crisis*, M.G. Hurtig, Edmonton, 1971.
    Walter Stewart, *Shrug: Trudeau in Power*, New Press, Toronto, 1971.
30. Gerard Pelletier, *The October Crisis*, trans. by Joyce Marshall, McClelland and Stewart, Toronto, 1971.

Index